CHRISTIAN HEROES: THEN & NOW

ELISABETH ELLIOT

Joyful Surrender

CHRISTIAN HEROES: THEN & NOW

ELISABETH ELLIOT

Joyful Surrender

JANET & GEOFF BENGE

YWAM
PUBLISHING
P.O. BOX 55787 / SEATTLE, WA 98155

YWAM Publishing is the publishing ministry of Youth With A Mission (YWAM), an international missionary organization of Christians from many denominations dedicated to presenting Jesus Christ to this genera- tion. To this end, YWAM has focused its efforts in three main areas: (1) training and equipping believers for their part in fulfilling the Great Com- mission (Matthew 28:19), (2) personal evangelism, and (3) mercy ministry (medical and relief work).

For a free catalog of books and materials, call (425) 771-1153 or (800) 922-2143. Visit us online at www.ywampublishing.com.

Elisabeth Elliot: Joyful Surrender

Published by YWAM Publishing
a ministry of Youth With A Mission
P.O. Box 55787, Seattle, WA 98155-0787

Library of Congress Cataloging-in-Publication Data
Benge, Janet, 1958–
    Elisabeth Elliot : joyful surrender / by Janet and Geoff Benge.
        p. cm.—(Christian heroes)
    Includes bibliographical references.
    ISBN 978-1-57658-513-9 (pbk.)
    1. Elliot, Elisabeth. 2. Missionaries—Ecuador—Biography. 3. Missionar-
ies—United States—Biography. I. Benge, Geoff, 1954– II. Title.
    BV2853.E3E44 2010
    266′.0237308092—dc22
    [B]   2010005801

Unless otherwise noted, Scripture quotations are taken from the Revised Standard Version of the Bible, Copyright 1946, 1952, 1971 by the Division of Christian Education of the National Council of the Churches of Christ in the U.S.A. Used by permission.

ISBN 978-1-57658-513-9 (paperback)
ISBN 978-1-57658-594-8 (e-book)

Fourth printing 2020

Printed in the United States of America

CHRISTIAN HEROES: THEN & NOW

Available in paperback, e-book, and audiobook formats. Unit study curriculum guides are available for select biographies.

www.YWAMpublishing.com

Ecuador

Central Oriente

N

Rio Napo

Shandia

Hacienda Ila

Arajuno

Palm Beach

Rio Curaray

Site of gift drop
to Waorani

Road from Quito
and Ambato

Tiwaeno

Rio Villano

Shell Mera

Villano

Puyupungu

Mt. Sangay

Macuma

Rio Pastaza

Contents

Chapter 1

She Could Not Turn Back Now

Before long you will all be dead and eaten by vultures!"

Elisabeth Elliot, or Betty, as most people called her, listened carefully to the words of Maruja, a Quichua Indian woman held captive for a year by a neighboring tribe. Betty and a group of others were on their way to the tribe's settlement for the first time.

"But did you learn to love them?" Betty pressed, hoping for some sign of hope and encouragement.

Maruja shook her head. "The women, yes, but not the men. They are fierce. You cannot love them."

Betty felt a chill run down her spine at the young Indian woman's words.

Like Maruja, Betty's life had been touched by the fierceness of this tribe. When Maruja was taken

captive, her husband was killed—speared to death—
by the attackers. And thirty-three months before,
beside the very river they were about to set out on
in canoes, Betty's husband and four other missionary men had been speared to death by the same tribe.
Both women understood what it was like to have
someone you love taken away in what seemed to be
a senseless act of violence.

Betty pondered Maruja's words. Was she doing
the right thing? After all, Maruja had spent a whole
year with the tribe. She knew them better than anyone. And now she was telling Betty and her traveling
companions that if they went ahead with their plan,
the men of the tribe would kill them.

It was a not an easy choice. Betty felt the cold
edge of fear. Yes, she had to admit there was a good
chance that she could be speared to death just as her
husband had been.

Yet she also felt a strange peace—almost exhila-
rating. This was the culmination of all Betty had
worked and prayed for during the past several years.
This was what her husband had given his life for.
This was her destiny. She could not turn back now.

At dawn the group set out in canoes down the Curaray River, following it to the Añangu River, which
they then followed upstream to the Tiwaeno River.
Finally the river became so shallow the canoes could
go no farther, and the travelers set out on foot through
the jungle. It took them two days, but eventually, late
in the afternoon, they rounded a bend in the trail, and
there was the settlement, a small cluster of thatched

huts set in a clearing. An Indian man, naked except for a strip of cotton cloth tied around his waist, stood on a log and watched as they approached, and several women stood at the entrances to the huts. They all stared as the group approached their village.

Betty breathed deeply as she walked past the man and into the village. Would she feel a sharp blow to her back next? She was living out one of those life-or-death tales she used to hear as a child back in Germantown, Pennsylvania. She recalled how she would sit at the dining room table mesmerized as she listened to visiting missionaries tell astonishing tales of faith in action. How far away that world now seemed.

Chapter 2

An Orderly Home

The year was 1934. Seven-year-old Betty Howard peered out the upstairs window of her bedroom in Germantown, Pennsylvania. Icicles hung off the clothesline in the backyard, and the flower garden was completely covered with a foot of snow. Since it was Saturday, Betty chose to put on her winter play clothes. Each child in the family had three sets of clothes: one for playing, one for school, and one to wear all day on Sunday.

After dressing, Betty put on her slippers and headed downstairs to help her mother fix breakfast. She was surprised to find her Aunt Alice standing by the stove, stirring a pot of oatmeal.

"Hello, young lady," Aunt Alice said in a soothing voice. "I guess you are wondering where your parents are. They're at the hospital getting a new baby—and during the coldest snap we've had in years, no less."

Betty plunked herself down on a chair. The baby was on its way!

"I'm sure you've been praying for a little sister," Aunt Alice continued.

Betty nodded. At age seven she was sandwiched between two brothers—Philip, who was ten, and Dave, who was six—and she certainly didn't think she needed another brother.

After breakfast, the three children did their morning chores, with Betty washing the dishes and wiping the counters. Betty had just about finished her chores when she heard the sound of breaking glass. She ran to investigate and found Dave staring at a broken window in the front room. He had been playing with the window sash, which was propped up with a stick. The window had fallen suddenly, shattering the glass into a thousand pieces.

"I was trying to open it," Dave stammered, "and it fell down and broke."

Aunt Alice entered the room and assessed the situation. "Step away from the jagged glass, children. Dave, go and get a broom."

Frigid air swirled around the room, and Betty gave an involuntary shudder while Aunt Alice went off to call a repairman. Unfortunately, the repairman could not come until later in the afternoon, and the temperature in the house was beginning to plummet. Betty and her brothers soon discovered that the warmest place in the house was right beside the heat register, where the three children camped out under a blanket. Now Betty wished for two things: first, that the baby would be born so that her parents could come home, and second, that the repairman would show up soon and fix the window.

Sometime around midday, the telephone rang and Aunt Alice answered it. A broad smile lit up her face as she exclaimed, "How wonderful! Thank the Lord everything went fine."

After she hung up the phone, Aunt Alice hugged Betty. "Your prayers have been answered. You have a baby sister, and her name is Virginia Anne Howard."

Betty smiled, though she could hardly imagine how a baby would fit into family life. Babies, Betty had observed, were noisy and unpredictable, and the Howard household was just the opposite. Everything in the house was done in an orderly, on-time manner. As Betty thought about it, she realized that her mother added adverbs to everything they did. The children weren't just to get dressed in the morning, but they were to get dressed *quickly*—no daydreaming allowed. They descended the stairs *noiselessly*, ate their breakfast *punctually* and *cheerfully*, brushed their teeth *vigorously*, and tucked in their bed sheets *meticulously*.

Betty's parents, Katherine and Philip Howard, lived by the same rules they expected their children to follow. In the Howard home, everything had a place, and the children were expected to return things to their proper place when they were done with them.

Betty marveled that even the pencils in the pencil box on her father's desk were all sharp and lay facing in the same direction, and the writing pads were always in perfect alignment with the corner of the desk.

Finally the repairman arrived and replaced the broken glass in the window. The children crawled out from under the blanket by the heat register as the house once again began to warm up.

Soon everything was back to normal, and Ginny, as everyone called the new baby, arrived to a warm and welcoming home. However, things at the house did not return to the way they had been before. Soon after Ginny's arrival, a round of sickness hit the Howard household. The health department required that all houses with sick people in them display a sign forbidding anyone but the breadwinner from entering or leaving them. And so a yellow quarantine sign was hung on the Howards' front door.

No one in the house was spared. The first round of sickness involved Betty's father, and then Betty came down with tonsillitis. Soon after, her brother Philip contracted the measles. A woman from church was given special permission to come to the house and help Mrs. Howard with all the extra work that a new baby and three sick people produced.

No sooner had Betty recovered than she, Philip, and their mother came down with the mumps. Instead of being cooped up in bed in her room, Betty longed to be outside playing Kick the Can or building a house from leftover cardboard and old blankets. Thanks to her good imagination, she escaped the four walls of her bedroom by reading and rereading her favorite books: *Winnie the Pooh, Peter Rabbit,* and *Sir Knight of the Splendid Way.*

As the days wore on, Betty's mother bought her a large scrapbook and several old copies of the *Saturday Evening Post*. Betty spent hours cutting out pictures from the old magazines and pasting them into the scrapbook. She especially liked studying the children in the Campbell Soup Kids advertisements.

Slowly the children began to recover from their illnesses, and then they all—including Betty for a second time—came down with tonsillitis. The doctor ordered that surgery be performed to remove each child's tonsils. Betty was not worried about the operation; she was just relieved that her very sore throat would at last start to feel better.

Throughout this time, Betty's parents tried to keep up the family routine as much as possible. Certain things, like morning and evening prayer devotions, could not be overlooked and continued with whoever was well enough to go downstairs and join in.

The Howard household thrived on routine, and devotions had been the same for as long as Betty could remember. In the morning after breakfast, the family would meet in the living room. Mr. Howard would lead the family in the singing of a hymn—a different one each morning until they had sung their way in an orderly manner through the entire hymnal. He and Betty's mother took turns playing the piano for accompaniment as they all sang. Then Betty's father would read a page or so from *Hurlbut's Story of the Bible,* after which everyone would kneel as Mr. Howard prayed for each person in turn. Lastly, they recited the Lord's Prayer together. Each evening Mr. Howard would read a portion of the Bible as the family sat around the dinner table.

On the days when Betty was too ill to come downstairs for meals, her father would come up to her room to pray for her in the morning and in the evening. He also always sang a hymn. Betty especially liked "Jesus, Tender Shepherd, Hear Me" and often hummed it as she drifted off to sleep.

By the time the entire Howard family was well again and the yellow sign could be taken down from the front door, it was late August. Betty was delighted to be able to go outside again and was especially glad to have some girl friends to play with. She had soon learned that although she now had a baby sister, that sister was not yet any fun to play with.

Knowing that summer would be over soon, Betty spent as much time as her mother would allow playing with her best friend, Essie. Until now, Betty had tried to do everything a good girl should do. Her father was the associate editor of the *Sunday School Times* and superintendent of their local Sunday school, and at home Betty heard a constant stream of Bible stories and prayers. But suddenly she was gripped with the idea of doing something really bad. She ran through the Ten Commandments in her head and came up with the idea that stealing would be the easiest way for her to have a sinful adventure.

Just as it was time to leave Essie's house one day, Betty spotted a brand new Mickey Mouse watch on top of the bottom banister of the stairs. "Let the adventure begin!" she told herself as she snatched the watch up and put it into her pocket.

Essie came skipping down the stairs, and the two girls said goodbye to each other. Betty was elated at how easy it had been to steal something. But her elation soon faded. As she walked down the street, she took the watch from her pocket and studied it. It had a picture of a mouse on the face, with long arms that were the hour and minute hands. Three more mice at the bottom of the face showed the seconds ticking away. This was the first time Betty had ever seen a watch with a cartoon on its face, and she was fascinated by it. Then she thought about how she had acquired the watch, and she felt as though someone had just punched her in the stomach.

What have I done? Betty asked herself. *Why did I steal the watch? It was Essie's. What kind of person would steal something from a friend?* She answered herself, *A really, really bad person, and I don't like that feeling at all.*

Soon Betty's conscience weighed so heavily on her that she stopped walking. She knew she should go back and return the watch, but she was terrified that she would run into Essie or her mother. Still, Betty could not stand the awful feeling inside, so she ran back to Essie's house and placed the watch on the back doorstep. Then she fled home.

That night Betty thought about what she had done. She had felt a quick thrill taking the watch, but the agony afterward had not been worth it. The verse her father often quoted from the Bible came to mind: "There is a way which seems right to a man, but its end is the way to death" (Proverbs 14:12). Yes, she'd had fun and adventure for a minute or two, but it wasn't fun in the long run. She went to sleep grateful that she'd at least had the courage to return the watch to Essie's house. She hoped and prayed that someone found it before it got stepped on.

At school Betty started third grade and was obliged to take sewing class. She hated having to go home and ask her parents for money to buy the necessary fabric for the sewing projects—even if it cost only twenty cents. (At the time, the United States was in the grip of the Great Depression, and money everywhere, including in the Howard household, was in short supply. Nonetheless, Betty's parents tithed on all the money they received. And from the money they tithed, a collection of dimes was kept in the drawer of the small table by the front door. The children were instructed to give a dime to each person who came to the door begging.)

As December approached, Betty looked forward to her birthday on the twenty-first, and then to Christmas. Christmas was a fun time for the Howard children. Early in the morning the children would pile onto their parents' bed and open the stocking they had found hanging on the end of their beds. While the stockings were mostly filled with practical things like bars of soap and pencils, they also included chocolate coins wrapped in gold foil. Betty loved the taste of the chocolate as it melted in her mouth. After breakfast and devotions, the family would gather around the Christmas tree to open presents. However, something happened early in December that year that took away much of Betty's joyful anticipation.

The Howard home was always open to missionaries and visiting speakers. In fact, even though the country was in the midst of the Great Depression and Betty's father had taken two pay cuts, the Howards were always the family who fed and boarded any Christian speakers who came through town.

Betty loved to read the guestbook her mother kept on the polished wooden table just inside the front door. The first entry in the book had been made shortly after her parents had married and set up home as missionaries with the Belgian Gospel Mission in Brussels, Belgium. The Howards had lived in Belgium for five years. Betty had been born there and was five months old when her parents returned to the United States for furlough. Her parents had fully intended to return to Belgium for a second term as missionaries, but Philip Howard's uncle, Charley Trumbull, asked Philip to consider joining the staff of the *Sunday School Times.* In the end Mr. Howard took the position, and the family bought a small house in Germantown. Since that time, many missionaries bound for Brussels and other cities and villages scattered around the world had passed through their house and signed the guestbook.

One of Betty's favorite visitors to the house was the Reverend Charles Scott. Mr. Scott and his wife, Clara, were missionaries in China, and he had taken a special interest in Betty. When he returned to China, he sent Betty Chinese candies, tiger skin slippers, and a paper fan. Not only that, he wrote her letters about his own daughter, who was also called Betty. Betty Scott, who Betty recalled had once stayed in their house with her father, had graduated from Moody Bible College and joined her parents as a missionary in Tsingteh, a small town in the east of China.

Betty Scott eventually married a missionary, John Stam, and in his last letter Charles Scott reported that the couple had just had a baby, whom they named Helen. It was easy for Betty Howard to put herself in the shoes of Betty Stam, since Charles Scott's letters were so vivid and lively. Betty secretly hoped that one day God would call her to be a missionary in some far-off place. How wonderful it would be to write the letters and live the adventures instead of just reading about them! So it came as a total shock to Betty when her mother called her into the parlor one afternoon in early December when she came home from school.

"Betty," she began, "I have something very difficult to tell you."

Betty stared at her mother. She had never seen her so sad.

"You remember Betty Stam and her father, the Reverend Scott?" Katherine Howard asked her daughter.

Betty nodded, of course she did.

"The Lord has called Betty and her husband John home to be with Him."

Betty struggled with the meaning of what she had just heard. *Calling home* was about dying, wasn't it? "What happened?" she asked.

Her mother folded her hands, and Betty could see big tears falling into her lap. "They were killed by Communists in China. Their little girl Helen is all right."

Betty did not know what to say. She thought of the baby growing up without parents and of poor Mr. Scott and his wife.

Later, as Betty listened to the adults around her discuss the murders, she was able to piece together more of the story. On December 6, John and Betty Stam had been arrested in their home by Communist fighters and forced to march with their three-month-old baby to Miaosheo, a town about twelve miles away. Two days later the Stams were marched through the streets of Miaosheo on their way to be executed. When a Chinese Christian man stepped forward and protested against what the Communists were doing, he, too, was arrested and marched off to be executed with the Stams. A short time afterward, John and Betty Stam were beheaded. Before her death, Betty had managed to hide baby Helen in a sleeping bag. The baby was found two days later by a Chinese pastor and returned to her grandparents, the Scotts, in Shanghai.

The details were shocking and sad to Betty. It was hard for her nearly eight-year-old mind to grasp how such a thing could happen. And so she passed a somber Christmas thinking about the Stams' baby, Helen, and what life would now be like for her without parents.

The year 1935 rolled around with some good news. Betty's mother was pregnant again and expecting a baby in July. As summer approached, Betty began to look forward both to the arrival of a new brother or sister and to going with the family to stay at Gale Cottage in New Hampshire. She planned to have a lot more fun this summer than the previous one, most of which she had spent sick in bed.

Chapter 3

Gale Cottage

Betty stowed her small leather suitcase in the string shelf above her bed and lay down. A big smile spread across her face as she felt the train vibrate and slowly pull forward. A whistle blasted through the air as the *Bar Harbor Express* gathered steam. Betty peered out the window of the Pullman coach and into the night. The Philadelphia station was alive with activity—men carrying parcels, women wheeling babies and studying timetables. Betty loved the swirl of activity around her, almost as much as she loved the anticipation of arriving at her favorite place on earth—Gale Cottage, in the foothills of New Hampshire's White Mountains, about six hundred miles up the train tracks.

Soon the train settled into a steady clickity-clack rhythm, and Betty watched the dark outlines of the backs of houses and factory buildings fly by in puffs of steam and smoke. Occasionally a live ember would streak by the window like a comet, escaping from the huge funnel on the locomotive. Before long, a tired Betty pulled down the blind and settled into her compact bed.

Betty was awakened in the early hours of the morning by the jerking of the Pullman car. She opened the blind and looked out. A brakeman with his lantern was standing by the side of the track, signaling the engineer with his hands. Betty knew it could mean only one thing: they had reached New Haven, Connecticut, and the train was being split into two trains. The *Bar Harbor Express* would continue on to Boston and then on into Maine, while the other half of the train, with its own steam locomotive and the Howard family aboard, would head north into New Hampshire. After jolting backward and forward, the train finally pulled away from the New Haven station. Betty soon settled back to sleep, excited to know that when she awoke she would be in a whole new place.

Betty woke to the sound of the hissing of steam as the train slowed down, followed by the sound of screeching brakes. She pulled up the blind and waited for the sign bearing the station's name to come into view. Concord. It wouldn't be long before they got to Littleton.

Betty climbed out of bed and dressed quickly so that she could spend the last half hour of the journey staring out the window. Just as she settled into her seat to take in the unfolding scenery, Betty's father ducked his head into her compartment. "How did you sleep?" he asked.

Betty grinned. "Just great! How about Mother and the baby?" The baby she was referring to was Thomas, the newest addition to the Howard family, born three weeks earlier.

"They did pretty well. Tommy fussed a little. Your mother will need a good rest when she gets to the cottage. Ginny slept right though. I guess she likes the rocking of the train," Philip Howard said.

The Howard family was standing ready to disembark when the train pulled to a stop at the Littleton station. As she climbed down from the Pullman car, Betty caught a glimpse of her grandfather. She waved vigorously at him, and he waved back.

Once they were all seated in her grandfather's Buick, Betty looked around. Everything was perfect. The weather was much cooler here in northern New Hampshire, and the constant traffic of Germantown and Philadelphia was far behind. Even the trees here were different—tall pines, wide-branching spruce, and white cedar. Best of all, an assortment of Howard family members would be waiting to greet them at the cottage.

The eight-mile drive to the cottage went quickly. As they drove, her grandfather quizzed the children on the names of the mountains that loomed in the distance: Lafayette, Bald Peak, Cannon, Kinsman, and Bluff. Betty remembered them all, and their names sounded like those of old friends to her.

Soon the Buick was click-clacking its way across the Gale River Bridge. Betty craned her neck to see, and joy swept over her when she spotted the two brick chimneys. Then the car turned into the driveway. The cottage looked just the same as she remembered. It was a two-story structure with a huge attic. The bottom story was built with large slabs of spruce, while the upper story and attic were clad in cedar shingles. A wide veranda ran all the way around the house, and standing on the veranda was Betty's grandmother waving a welcome. The table in front of her was already set, as Betty knew it would be, so they could all enjoy a delicious breakfast together outside.

Betty took a deep breath as she ran around the house. The place still smelled the same. She recognized the scent of the sturdy spruce timbers mixed with the wood smoke that permeated them. She found the little cart she remembered playing with two years before and popped her head into the kitchen, which was a separate building behind the house. She recalled her mother explaining to her that the kitchen had to be separate in case of fire.

Breakfast on the veranda turned out to be even better than Betty remembered. Her grandmother urged her to have a second helping of pancakes. "You're growing up fast!" she exclaimed. "You'll be as tall as your father soon."

Betty felt herself blush. It was true: she was growing fast. Her dresses were down to the last turn of their hems, and her socks no longer reached all the way to her knees. She was a good head taller and ganglier than the other girls her age.

Once the table had been cleared and the dishes washed in a huge enamel bowl, the Howard children were free to explore.

Gale Cottage couldn't have been more different from the Howards' house in Germantown. Back there Betty knew every item in every cupboard. But here at the cottage, every drawer, cupboard, or box in the attic could hold a wonderful surprise. Betty found a mummified human foot, which her Uncle Will—the owner of the cottage—had brought back from Egypt. Uncle Will had been collecting artifacts for the Metropolitan Museum in New York, and somehow this foot had never made it as far as New York. The same box that held the mummified foot also held a mechanical bear, an ancient black lace parasol, and a music box, all with stories of their own.

A shelf in the back parlor held a stereopticon, a contraption that allowed a person to look into it and see hand-retouched photographs in 3-D. The pictures were of sparkling ice caves and gushing waterfalls. Glass cases filled with pinned-down butterflies and moths also sat on the shelf. Using such "props," Betty and her brothers acted out wonderful stories that they made up.

Betty loved the fact that the cottage held many family stories. An ash-wood paddle hung on the wall, which her father had brought with him from Maine the summer before he married her mother. He had been a camp counselor at Camp Allagash on Moosehead Lake and asked one of the guides to make the paddle for him and inscribe the initials PH, for Philip Howard, on one side, and KG, for Katherine Gillingham, on the other. Betty thought the paddle was very romantic, and she liked to imagine her mother visiting her father at the cottage and being presented with the paddle.

In the attic were two worn leather-bound books written by Betty's great-grandfather, Henry Clay Trumbull. Her great-grandfather had been a minister in the Congregational Church and had served as the chaplain of the Tenth Connecticut Regiment during the Civil War. At one point he was even captured and held in a Confederate prison. Although poor health kept him from receiving a formal education beyond the age of fourteen, he had managed to earn three honorary degrees, one each from Yale, Lafayette, and the University of New York.

Betty's grandfather had told her that Henry Clay Trumbull was highly respected by his regiment during the Civil War. Not only did her great-grandfather preach eloquent sermons and remain dedicated to the men, but he also was a courageous man who would get into the trenches with the rest of the men and rally them on in the thick of battle. After the Civil War he had gone on to become the founder and editor of the *Sunday School Times* and had written two books: *The Knightly Soldier,* a biography of his Civil War friend Adjutant Henry Ward Camp, and *War Memories of an Army Chaplain.* When she heard the stories of such relatives, Betty felt that her roots were as deep as the spruce tree in the front yard of Gale Cottage.

Each day at the cottage was an adventure. While Betty's mother stayed home most of the time with Ginny and the new baby, her father took the other children out into the mountains to hike. He was a wonderful observer of nature, often standing for an hour or more perfectly still with his hands clasped behind his back. Betty loved to hear him imitate bird-calls and laughed when the birds answered him back as if he were one of their own.

Sometimes they hiked for miles, right to the top of one of the peaks, where Betty was rewarded with breathtaking vistas of the surrounding countryside. And no walk was complete without talking about the Bible and how God had made such an amazing world for them all to enjoy.

Aunt Anne, Betty's father's younger sister, often took Betty for long walks. Going with Aunt Anne was a different kind of adventure, one that Betty especially loved. Together they would ramble through the valleys, stopping to pick wildflowers, which they would bring back to the cottage to press into a small scrapbook. Soon Betty had quite a collection that included such flowers as quaker-ladies, wild orchids, devil's paintbrush, goldenrod, and butter-and-eggs. Sometimes in the evenings she would take out her scrapbook and carefully study each flower.

Also, Aunt Anne would rig up a large white sheet on the veranda and place a lantern behind it. The light would attract moths, which would fly into the sheet. Betty and Aunt Anne would eagerly catch the moths to preserve the next day.

The whole Howard family loved nature, or so it seemed to Betty. Aunt Anne had told Betty that her great-great-aunt Annie Trumbull Slosson had been a writer and well-known entomologist. In fact, according to Aunt Anne, Annie Slosson had documented over one hundred previously unstudied insects, each of which now bore the suffix *slossonii*.

At night, the family gathered around the huge fire in the fireplace in the living room for hymn singing and prayer. Sometimes Betty's father would sit in a rocking chair and tell the children stories about his adventures before he was married.

The stories Betty loved best revolved around her father's stint as assistant to George Davis, the director of the Pocket Testament League. Philip Howard had not been called up for service in the Great War because he had the use of only one eye. Instead, he volunteered to travel throughout the western United States as far as San Francisco and south to the Mexican border. He would meet with soldiers in training camps and hand out free copies of the New Testament for the soldiers to take with them when they shipped out overseas to fight. He and George Davis gave out thousands of copies of the New Testament. They also prayed with the men, and Betty's dad would play the piano while the men gathered to sing hymns.

The western deserts, with their sand, cactuses, snakes, and coyotes, came alive to Betty as her father talked about camping out under open skies. After he had described San Francisco, Betty longed to see the place, with ferryboats coming and going and misty fog swirling across the bay.

Sometimes, though not often, Philip Howard told the children the story of how he came to lose the use of his left eye. During the summer when he was thirteen years old, he went with his parents to D. L. Moody's conference center in Northfield, Massachusetts. On the Fourth of July, his father had forbidden him to have fireworks to celebrate the holiday. But Philip managed to get his hands on some anyway— dynamite caps. He went to a nearby farm and asked the farmer to help him fire off the caps. The farmer agreed, and they put the caps on the ground, lit the fuse, and retreated to watch the explosion. But there was no explosion. So they walked back to the dynamite caps and the farmer kicked them. Immediately the caps exploded, and in the process a shard of copper pierced Philip's left eye. The family made a rush overnight train trip back to Philadelphia, where the doctor declared that Philip was lucky he had not lost the use of both eyes. Mr. Howard always ended the story with a few words on the importance of obeying your parents and not doing things your own way.

Betty's mother also had stories to tell that ignited Betty's imagination. One cool evening she told about her great-grandfather, Frank Gillingham, who had been an officer in the Union Army. Frank had fought at Antietam, the bloodiest battle of the Civil War, but had managed to come through the battle unscathed.

When President Lincoln was assassinated, Frank was assigned the task of escorting the President's body back to Illinois. Betty's mother described how the funeral train would stop at every town along the way and how Great-Grandfather Gillingham would brush the cinders off the dead President's face and prepare Mr. Lincoln for a viewing.

Just before summer recess, Betty had been learning at school about President Lincoln. The idea that her family had real, tangible links with such an important person from the past thrilled her. Sometimes when she lay awake at night listening to the swish of the wind through the pine trees and the gurgling of the river in the distance, she wondered how her life would turn out. Would she have amazing stories to tell her own children?

Chapter 4

Adventurous Aspirations

Betty hated to leave Gale Cottage and all the wonderful activities she had been involved in there. But on the train trip back to Philadelphia, her mother told her something that filled her with excitement: the family was going to buy a car! Betty could hardly believe what she was hearing. She tried to imagine how different things would be with their very own car.

Sure enough, within weeks of getting back from New Hampshire, Betty's father drove home a 1932 Plymouth sedan with yellow-spoked wheels. Betty couldn't help but notice the way her mother's face lit up at the sight of the vehicle. "What a wonder!" her mother said. "It takes me back to when I was a young woman in 1917." Betty laughed. She had seen the photo of her mother perched behind the heavy steering wheel of the Buick Roadster that Grandfather Gillingham had bought her. She remembered her mother telling about all the extra attention she had received from boys wanting to take a ride in the car. Betty liked to think of her mother as a daring young woman, wrapped in a raccoon skin coat and wearing a beaver hat tied firmly on her head, cruising around town in her Buick.

Soon Betty learned that another big change was in store for the family: they were moving. Yes, with five children, the Howards' home in Germantown had become too cramped. Betty and the boys were used to the confined space, but the fact was that the house at 103 West Washington Lane had very few places to play. The house had a pocket-sized yard, and the place was dark and gloomy inside.

The family piled into the Plymouth for the first look at their new home, which was sixteen miles away across the Tacony-Palmyra Bridge. Betty's brothers were fascinated by the huge arch that formed the bridge's center span and the bump in the surface that was the center of the drawbridge section of the structure. Philip Howard explained to his children that the river beneath them was the Delaware and that the state line ran right along the river, so that in driving across the bridge they had passed from Pennsylvania to New Jersey.

Finally Betty's father turned the car onto a street in Moorestown, New Jersey. "There it is!" he said with a flourish. "Number 29 East Oak Avenue."

In front of them on the corner stood a stately three-story house. Betty could hardly believe it. Compared to the house in Germantown it looked like a mansion. As Betty soon discovered, the place had seventeen rooms—a room for each of them and still lots left over. A veranda stretched along two sides of the house, which was surrounded by a big yard with a dogwood, a poplar, and a beech tree growing in front. Betty knew from the moment she set eyes on the new house that she was going to be very happy living in Moorestown.

Of course, moving from Pennsylvania to New Jersey meant a change of school and making new friends, which was difficult for a shy girl like Betty. However, their big yard was a huge attraction, and Betty soon made some friends. A florist business with a row of greenhouses was located across the street from the house. The florist regularly discarded large wooden boxes in which flowers had been delivered to the business. He allowed the children to take the boxes to play with. Back in the yard of the Howard house, the children used the boxes to build small playhouses, in which they occupied themselves for hours on end.

Even though the Howards were now farther away from the *Sunday School Times* headquarters, missionaries continued to visit and stay and regularly regaled the children with their stories. Russell Abel from the South Pacific Mission thrilled them with stories of having to flee from cannibals, while L. L. Legters spoke about Indian tribes in Mexico that no one outside of that country even knew existed.

A single woman, Helen Yost, a missionary among the Indians of Arizona, opened Betty's mind to the importance of Bible translation work.

One visitor who made an impression on Betty during this time was an Armenian woman named Arousiag Stepanian. Around the Howards' dinner table one evening, Arousiag recounted what happened to her and her family in 1915 at the hands of the Turks. She was twelve years old at the time and lived with her family in the city of Brousa, near Constantinople (now Istanbul). But the Turks decided to move all Armenians out of the area.

Arousiag's family and all the other Armenians around were forced to pack their belongings and leave their homes behind. What followed was a harrowing journey of many months. Along the way Arousiag's parents died, leaving her and her three sisters all alone. The four sisters stuck together, supporting one another. Many people urged them to convert to Islam and save themselves, but the girls held firmly to their Christian beliefs.

Then one day the Stepanian sisters, along with many other Armenians, were forced to cross a river, not at the usual ford but at a dangerously swift place with steep sides running down to the water. The two younger sisters were assisted safely across to the other side, and then Arousiag's older sister made it across. Finally Arousiag was able to make it to the other side of the river. But once on the other side, the two older girls could not find their two younger sisters. As they searched for their sisters, a soldier stopped the two older girls and tried to forcibly take them into his harem. Arousiag resisted and was cut by the man's sword before he threw her into the river.

"In the plunge I struck the river bottom," Arousiag said. Betty sat spellbound listening to the story. "When I came to the surface I tried to swim, though I had never been taught. Somehow I was floating with the current. I heard a rifle shot and, immediately after, a cry from Pailazou [her older sister]: 'Goodbye, Arousiag, goodbye!' I was struggling in the water and was almost drowning, so I could not see what happened on the bank. Had Pailazou attempted to escape? Was she wounded or killed? I do not know to this day."

Nor did Arousiag ever see her two younger sisters again. Soon after crossing the river, many of the Armenians were massacred by the Turks. Perhaps her sisters were killed in the massacre, or perhaps they escaped. Arousiag would never know.

Arousiag carried on with her story, telling how she didn't drown but was washed downstream until she was able to crawl from the river. Soon afterward, a nomadic Arab family captured her and took her as their servant. To disguise her Armenian identity, the family dressed Arousiag in Arab clothing and tattooed her forehead, cheeks, and chin in traditional designs. (Betty could clearly see the unusual marks on her face.) For eighteen months Arousiag served as the Arab family's servant, traveling with them as they moved from grazing place to grazing place following their herds.

Betty herself was twelve years old, the same age Arousiag had been at the time of her ordeal, and she wondered how or even whether she could survive such a harrowing experience. But Arousiag had survived, and she spoke freely of the power of her Christian faith to help her through the terrible ordeal. Betty stored away Arousiag's example inside.

For now Betty's life was stable and quiet, lacking any kind of adventure. Life in Moorestown had fallen into a pleasant routine for her. She did well at school, made new friends, and enjoyed her summers at Gale Cottage in New Hampshire. It was when she was thirteen, just after Jim, her last sibling, was born, that Betty turned her mind to the matter of Christianity. Of course, she had always considered herself a Christian, but now as a teenager she was asking questions that hadn't occurred to her before. She wanted to be sure she had her own faith and not just the faith of her parents.

At the time Betty was reading a newly published biography of Betty Stam, who had been murdered along with her husband by a brigade of Chinese Communists. Betty still fondly remembered the time Betty Stam and her parents had stayed at the Howards' house in Germantown. She also still vividly remembered the time when her mother told her of Betty and John Stam's murders. Having known Betty Stam made the biography come alive to Betty Howard. As she read, she came across a passage in which Betty Stam had written:

Lord, I give up all my own plans and purposes, all my own desires and hopes, and accept Thy will for my life. I give myself, my life, my all utterly to Thee to be Thine, forever. Fill me and seal me with Thy Holy Spirit. Use me as Thou wilt, work out Thy whole will in my life at any cost, now and forever.

Betty copied Betty Stam's prayer at the front of her Bible and read it often. And when she read it, she thought about Betty and her sacrifice.

In many ways it was easier for Betty to identify with the adult missionaries who came through their home than it was to make friends with the other girls in her class at public school. As she finished ninth grade, Betty began to feel more and more like an outsider. None of the girls in her class appeared to be interested in spiritual things, while Betty longed for the opportunity to build strong Christian friendships.

Great-Uncle Charley Trumbull, the general editor and owner of the *Sunday School Times*, inadvertently fueled Betty's aspirations for something better. On his return from a trip to Florida, Uncle Charley brought back the yearbook from a school for missionary children called the Hampden DuBose Academy, located in Orlando. Betty studied the exotic-looking green-tinted cover of the yearbook. She opened the book and read every word and then studied every photo. It all looked wonderful. The school was located on 105 acres of land, which included 40 acres of landscaped campus and 8 acres of orange groves. Classes were held in an old mansion. Betty could picture herself in the photos, sitting primly in the living room with its dark wood paneling, or gathering to sing around the piano. The outdoor photos captivated her too. In one photo, formally dressed boys and girls sat under huge oak trees draped with Spanish moss on the shore of a glistening lake. Class outings showed students laughing on the white-sand shores of their own island in the middle of a lake, bowling in the bowling alley, and wandering down a path ablaze with azaleas.

Betty also read about how Pierre DuBose, the school's founder and principal, had been a missionary child in China and had returned alone to the United States for high school. But things had not gone well for him with his schooling, and he vowed to establish a school where missionary children could feel cared for and loved—a real home away from home. The staff considered their careers a call from God, and although the school paid their room and board, each staff member had to trust that God would meet all of his or her other personal needs.

It all seemed so romantic to Betty, who begged her parents to allow her to get the rest of her high school education at the academy. As much as her parents may have wanted her to go, however, the fact was that they did not have the money to send her to the Hampden DuBose Academy.

Then Great-Uncle Charley died unexpectedly in 1941, and this changed many things for the Howard family. Betty's father became the general editor for the *Sunday School Times* and received a substantial raise in salary to go with the new position. As a result, the decision was made that Betty and her older brother Philip could both go to boarding school. Philip decided to attend the Prairie Bible Institute in Alberta, Canada, but Betty was firm in her desire to go to the Hampden DuBose Academy in Orlando at the beginning of the next academic year. Next year, she determined, *her* picture would be taken under those Spanish moss–laden oak trees.

On December 7, 1941, soon after Uncle Charley's death, the Howard family was as shocked as the rest of the country to learn of a massive Japanese air attack on Pearl Harbor in Hawaii. Many American servicemen had been killed in the attack, many aircraft had been destroyed, and ships had been sunk. Soon afterward President Franklin Roosevelt announced on the radio that the United States was now officially at war with Japan and Germany. America had finally entered the war that had been raging in Europe and parts of East Asia for over two years.

Despite the fact that the United States was now at war, in September 1942, fifteen-year-old Betty Howard stood on the platform of the Philadelphia Railway Station, clad in a beige felt hat, blue woolen dress, thick stockings, and brown pumps—all suitable attire for fall in New Jersey. She took a deep breath, and once she had climbed aboard the *Tamiami Champion* and found her berth, she looked out of the railway car window. Her whole family had come to see her off. As she peered out the window, Betty suddenly felt engulfed with the reality of the situation. For the first time she was leaving home—alone. None of her brothers or sisters were with her in the train car, and she was headed farther away from home than she had ever been in her life. Not only that, she would not see or talk to any of her family for nine long months. It was too far to travel home for Christmas or Easter and too expensive to make long-distance telephone calls. It was a sobering moment for Betty as the locomotive hissed and slowly pulled the train away from the station.

It was an overnight trip south on the train, and in Jacksonville, Florida, the *Tamiami Champion* was split in two, with one train going to Miami on Florida's east coast and the other train going to St. Petersburg on Florida's west coast. Betty rode aboard the train headed for St. Petersburg. As the train passed through central Florida, it stopped in Orlando.

With the sun up, Betty stared out the window at a landscape unlike any she had ever seen before. There wasn't a hill in sight, just flat land. Some of the land was pastureland with cows grazing on it, but much of the land was covered in spindly pine trees. Small lakes and swamps seemed to be everywhere. Betty cringed when she thought about the many alligators that probably inhabited the lakes and swamps.

Finally, in the early afternoon, the train came to a halt at Church Street Station in Orlando. Betty was anxious as she climbed down from the train, gripping her suitcases tightly. About ten other people were disembarking the train in Orlando, and Betty's stomach churned as she imagined what would happen if no one was there to meet her.

A blast of humid air enveloped Betty as she stepped onto the station platform. It felt to her like she had just walked into a steamy shower room, and her woolen dress clung to her. Betty looked around. Fortunately, it took only a minute to spot a tall, thin woman wearing a long, white dress. The woman had spotted Betty, too, and made a beeline for her.

"Hello," the woman said, beaming. "You must be Betty Howard. I'm Miss Andy. Welcome! We're so glad you are here!"

Betty smiled back. She hoped she looked glad to be there.

Miss Andy effortlessly took Betty's suitcases and walked to a nearby parked station wagon. She loaded the bags into the back of the vehicle and told Betty to climb into the front seat. "We call the car 'Long John,'" she said, smiling. "I expect you're a little bit overwhelmed right now, but I know you'll love the academy." Miss Andy beamed as she started up the station wagon and drove off. "Tell me, how was your train ride?"

Despite her shyness, Betty found herself chatting with Miss Andy as they drove along.

Soon Miss Andy pulled the station wagon into the driveway of a beautiful old mansion located south of downtown Orlando. Betty settled into the dorm and then went to explore her new surroundings. Instantly the pages of the yearbook came alive. There was the goldfish pond in front of the veranda, and Betty walked down the azalea path. The school enrolled children from first grade through twelfth grade, and sure enough, Betty soon came upon the little girls' playhouse. Several girls were treating their dolls to a tea party. They smiled at Betty and asked her name.

Coming from a large family, Betty felt right at home with all the different aged children. She was surprised, however, to learn that Miss Andy lived in the dorm with her and the three other girls in tenth grade.

Betty settled in quickly to school life and made friends with the other girls. Some of the students complained privately about the formal requirements of the school: learning how to serve and eat from a well-laid table, the rules of dating (which were practiced every Saturday night with a different date), and the correct way to do everything from tucking in the blankets on your bed to welcoming a guest. But Betty already knew most of this from her upbringing, and she thrived at the school.

Mrs. DuBose, the principal's wife, took a special interest in Betty and determined to help her overcome her shyness. The two of them spent many hours together sitting and talking on the veranda overlooking the lake. Mrs. DuBose introduced Betty to the writings of Amy Carmichael, a missionary from Northern Ireland who had gone to southern India and started a mission ministering to needy children. Amy had written nearly forty inspirational Christian books, which Betty found herself drawn to. The books were both comforting and challenging. Betty wondered whether she would ever be able to handle the kinds of sacrifices that were required of Amy Carmichael.

Mrs. DuBose urged Betty to join the debate team and put her writing talents to work as an editor of *Esse*, the school yearbook. Besides keeping up with her academic subjects, Betty soon found herself participating in intense debates and compiling the next edition of the yearbook, like the one she had spent so much of her time dreaming over before coming to the academy.

Chapter 5

Wheaton College

Betty looked out the railway car window as the train pulled away from Church Street Station. After nearly two years, she was leaving Orlando behind for good. It was May 1944, and she had just graduated from the Hampden DuBose Academy. As the train gathered steam, Betty thought back to her first trip to Florida. How timid and worried she had felt then—worried whether she would fit in, worried whether she would miss her family too much, worried whether she would like being in such a hot climate. Now it was all behind her. She had survived and thrived at the school. She was no longer the shy, timid girl she had been. Mrs. DuBose's tutelage had seen to that. Betty was as comfortable now playing the piano and singing in front of a group as she was standing and speaking to the same group. She had also done well at her academic subjects and had particularly enjoyed English, especially English composition.

Now it was time to look ahead. Betty already knew where she was headed next year. She'd been accepted at Wheaton College, where she hoped to complete her premedical degree. Wheaton College was an evangelical liberal arts college located in Wheaton, Illinois, about twenty-five miles west of Chicago. Betty's father was now a member of the board of trustees for the institution. This meant that Betty could attend school there for free. The Howard family still had to be careful with their money.

Betty had a wonderful reunion with her family upon her return from Florida and spent the summer with them in Moorestown and at Gale Cottage in New Hampshire. She particularly enjoyed her time at the cottage.

Her brothers and sisters seemed to have grown up while she had been away. Her older brother Phil had just completed a year of study at the National Bible Institute in New York and was engaged to a fellow student, Margaret Funderburk. Betty watched as the two of them planned their wedding and their lives together. Even though she was next in line chronologically to Phil, Betty doubted that she would be the next one to marry. It was difficult for her to imagine, since she had never even been on a serious date.

While her older brother planned his wedding, Betty had fun going fishing with her younger brothers

Tom and Jim, who were now nine and five years old. She marveled at the way the young boys loved to fish for hours on end. Betty also took long walks with her sister Ginny, an inquisitive eleven-year-old who wondered, as Betty had, what life had in store for her. Betty was able to pray with her and encouraged her to read systematically through the Bible.

As the summer of 1944 drew to a close, it was time for Betty to once again pack up her things and head back to school. Only this time she would be headed westward to Chicago, a place—like Orlando—she had never even visited before arriving there to attend school.

Once again Betty Howard departed Philadelphia by train. As the train rolled along heading west, Betty got her first taste of the Midwest. She was amazed at how flat, like Florida, the countryside was. The train pulled into the station in Chicago, a bustling and growing city set at the southern end of Lake Michigan. While Orlando had been a sleepy place, Chicago gave the impression that it never slept, that its energy was unbounded. In Chicago Betty switched to a local train that took her the rest of the way to Wheaton.

At the train station in Wheaton, a senior student assigned to help Betty settle in to school life met her, and together they took a taxi to Wheaton College.

The first thing Betty noticed as they drove onto the campus of the college was Blanchard Hall, a large, imposing limestone tower building with an expansive lawn in front of it. Behind Blanchard Hall were a number of other brick and stone buildings clustered around quadrangles. Betty was shown to her room on the fourth floor of one of these buildings, North Hall.

Betty was surprised at how crowded the rooms were. She soon found out why. Fifteen hundred students were enrolled in the college for the semester, but only three hundred of them were men. This was because so many young men of college age had been drafted into the military and were now overseas fighting in the war. As a result of this imbalance in numbers, the girls had to double up in rooms that were ordinarily single rooms. Betty's room had two beds, but only one dresser, one desk, and one wardrobe. Her roommate's father owned a department store, and it showed in the number of clothes her roommate had brought with her to Wheaton. Betty did the best she could to fit her few items of clothing into the wardrobe.

A woman named Catherine Cumming was a housemother at North Hall, and she and Betty became instant friends, despite the fact that Catherine was forty years older than Betty. Catherine was a caring person and a good listener who would offer helpful suggestions when Betty went to her with problems. Betty was impressed with Catherine's dedication to her faith and to the students under her care. In her Southern drawl, Catherine told Betty how she came from a very wealthy family in Georgia. Catherine's family, however, had disowned her and cut her off from her inheritance (which she said would have been several million dollars) because she had become a Christian. Catherine had found her way to Wheaton College, where she had served as housemother for many years. Betty was impressed by the story. She found herself drawn to people whose faith had cost them something.

One of Betty's first challenges after arriving at Wheaton was finding a part-time job so that she could earn spending money. She went to the college employment office, where she got a job working for Dr. Edman, the president of Wheaton College. Betty soon found herself cleaning at Westgate, the Edmans' residence, every other day and doing the ironing for the whole Edman family.

In the classroom, Betty soon learned that her academic training had not been as rigorous as some of the other students. She found note taking and organizing her time between various classes and assignments a challenge. However, Marcia Bell, who lived in the dorm room next to Betty's in North Hall, was brilliant at such matters. She helped Betty improve her note taking and the managing of her notebook and time. Before Betty knew it, lectures were no longer a drudgery of trying to keep up with the professor and write down everything of importance he or she said.

Eager to be a part of the fabric of campus life, Betty signed up to be a reporter on the college newspaper, *The Record*. However, when she arrived at the newspaper office, the number of junior and senior students hard at work preparing the next issue overwhelmed her. She wondered what she, as a freshman reporter, might have to offer these people, who seemed so competent at what they were doing. At first she just wanted to turn around and walk out the door. *I'll never be able to do this,* she told herself. But somehow she managed to overcome her fears, and soon she was busy contributing to the paper.

Betty always looked forward to visits from her father. He made regular trips to Wheaton College to attend board of trustee meetings, and when he came, he and Betty would eat together in the dining room and talk for hours.

Betty's first year at Wheaton began to roll by. She passed all her courses, but she realized that she did not want to continue her current course of study in premed. Instead she decided that the following year she would change her major to English.

As the 1944–45 school year drew to a close, Betty participated in a large event held at Soldier Field in Chicago. A new organization called Youth For Christ had just been formed, and the president of the organization was thirty-six-year-old Torrey Johnson, who had been pastor of Chicago's Midwest Bible Church. The stated mission of Youth For Christ was twofold. The first goal was revitalizing Americans' spiritual lives, bringing America back to God, the Bible, and the church. The second goal was the evangelization of the world. Even Betty had to admit that the goals were big, but Torrey seemed to be the kind of gifted leader who could make them a reality. To this end, Youth For Christ organized a large evangelistic rally to be held on Memorial Day 1945 at Soldier Field. A feature of the rally was to be a five-thousand-voice choir. When Betty heard an appeal at chapel service one morning for volunteers to be in the choir, she signed up.

Memorial Day 1945 dawned a cold, gray, overcast day. *Not the best weather for an outdoor rally,* Betty thought as she climbed aboard the bus that would take her and the other choir volunteers from Wheaton College to Soldier Field in downtown Chicago. At Soldier Field Betty took her place with the other choir members and waited for the audience to arrive. As she waited, Betty was amazed at the steady stream of people who filed into the stadium.

By the time the event started, seventy thousand people had packed into Soldier Field for the Youth For Christ rally. When it came the choir's turn to sing, Betty stood with the others and sang her heart out. Their voices blended together in a crescendo that filled and reverberated around the massive stadium. As the rally drew to a close, Torrey stood to preach to the crowd. He proved to be a more dynamic speaker than Betty could have imagined, and the large crowd sat motionless and spellbound as they listened to his words.

"Young folks, is He yours? Have you really been born again? Or are you hiding a heart full of sin behind the cloak of a lot of Scripture verses and other things? I wonder, if God took you right now, are you sure that you would go to heaven? If you are not, make sure tonight," Torrey challenged the crowd as the rally came to a close.

As the bus traveled back to Wheaton College, Betty reflected on what a wonderful experience the rally had been, especially when so many young people had come forward to accept Christ at the appeal Torrey had given at the end of his sermon.

Betty returned home to Moorestown for the summer. She had long talks with her brother Dave, who planned to join her at Wheaton College for the 1945–46 school year. Just as the two of them were preparing to leave for Illinois, World War II came to a close with the surrender of Japan on August 15, 1945. The whole of the United States exuberantly celebrated the victory.

Back at Wheaton College, Betty settled into her English classes. English came more naturally to her than science had. Still she found time for extracurricular activities, including becoming a member of the college debate squad.

Like the one before, the school year of 1945–46 sped by, as did the following year, her junior year. Betty continued to study hard, make good grades, and faithfully attend the Foreign Missions Fellowship. In December 1946, when Betty turned twenty, some of the women in the dorm threw a small birthday party for her, but there were no men in sight. Betty accepted the fact. She was taller than many of the men at college and naturally thin. She also had an intense personality and would rather talk theology than flirt. And although she would have liked to meet a man on campus to be her husband, she was not sure if that would happen. In fact, as she entered her twenties, Betty thought God might be calling her to go to the mission field as a single woman. The thought did not appeal to her, but she was willing to pray about it. One night in her journal she wrote, "Read about Henry Martyn of India, who had to choose between the woman he loved and the mission field. Shall I have to choose between marriage and mission?"

Chapter 6

An Interesting Man

Betty glanced up from her classic Greek history textbook and noticed a male student across the aisle. She had seen him before but had not paid much attention to him. She knew his name was Jim Elliot and that he was a year behind her, in the same class as her brother Dave. In fact Dave, who was on the college wrestling team, often talked about his friend Jim, but Betty had never been formally introduced. Now for a split second she wished she had.

Betty studied Jim's profile. He had a sloping forehead, lots of wavy, dark brown hair, broad shoulders, and the barrel chest of a wrestler. His clothes, however, didn't make him stand out from the rest of the class. He wore a sky blue sweater, a well-worn gabardine jacket, a bow tie, gray socks, and a sturdy pair of shoes. *Rather ordinary,* Betty thought. But she had to admit that there was something extraordinary about Jim Elliot. She noticed that even when sitting quietly studying, Jim possessed an aura of confidence, of—she struggled for the words—a kind of strength of conviction. In a fleeting moment, Betty decided she wanted to get to know Jim better.

Betty had never felt this curious about a young man before. She'd had a few dates here and there in high school, but that was boarding school, and everyone there had to pair up for formal nights. The boys had to politely ask the girls out, and the rules were that the girls could not refuse. It was hardly a system designed to foster romance, Betty concluded as she thought about it. But now she was in her third year of college, and she had been on fewer than a dozen dates the whole time she had been at Wheaton. None of them had been very inspiring—just a couple of campus concerts and a hayride one Thanksgiving. Since Wheaton College did not allow students to go to movies, that was not a dating option.

As Betty prayed that night, Jim Elliot's face kept coming into her mind. She tried to dismiss it. After all, she had given her life to God and agreed to "go into all the world" as a single missionary. She told herself she needed to stay focused on her studies, especially now. Betty had started Wheaton College thinking that God might be leading her to be a doctor, perhaps in Africa or some other place that required her to live in a grass hut. But as time went on, she felt a steady pull toward Bible translation work, and during her third year she changed her major from English to Greek.

She knew she had a lot of catch-up work to do if she was to graduate on schedule. Betty planned to take second-year Greek over the summer break and then work extra hard her senior year, combining her third and fourth years of Greek. As a result, she reasoned, she had little or no room in her life for the distraction of a boyfriend.

A week later Betty found herself once again sitting and watching Jim Elliot, only this time in a totally different context. She had gone to Alumni Gym to watch her brother Dave wrestle, but also wrestling that day was Jim Elliot, the India-rubber man, as he was known in wrestling circles. Betty could see how he got his nickname. No matter what sort of positional offense Jim's opponent seemed to apply, Jim was almost impossible to pin down on the mat. Betty was impressed by Jim's agility.

After the wrestling match, Betty quizzed Dave more on his friend. She soon learned that Jim was a man of definite opinions. He was from a Plymouth Brethren family from Oregon, and Dave told her that he knew the Bible better than any member of the Howard family. Betty found this hard to believe, but curiosity drove her to get to know Jim better.

Once Jim realized that Betty was Dave's sister, he often stopped to say hello to her after class. It was difficult for Betty to overcome her natural shyness around men, but she made every effort to be friendly.

Betty had less time to spare hanging around after class, especially as the Northwest Debating Championship loomed. Betty had joined the Wheaton

College debate squad during her sophomore year, and now as a junior she was going to compete in the debating championship. Of course, debating wasn't all about talking and persuasively putting forth your side of an argument. Before you got to that stage, a lot of study of the topic at hand needed to be done. The debate topic for the Northwest Debating Championship was Compulsory Arbitration. So, as well as being involved in all of her other studies, Betty, along with the other members of the debate squad, spent a lot of time in the library learning all she could about compulsory arbitration. She noted both the good and the bad things about it, since the squad did not know until the championship whether they would be arguing for the affirmative or the negative regarding the subject.

Even Betty had to admit that the subject of compulsory arbitration was dull and boring. Nonetheless, when it was her turn to speak, she argued passionately for the subject, and to the delight of her and her team members, their squad won the championship.

During the summer of 1947, Betty stayed at Wheaton College to take her second-year Greek course. The campus was completely different over the summer. Fewer students were around, and everyone ate in the same dining room instead of in separate ones. And since no clubs or extracurricular activities were going on, Betty was able to focus completely on the task at hand—passing the second-year Greek course in one summer. As she studied, from time to time

Betty found herself wondering what Jim Elliot might be doing back home in Oregon for the summer.

Betty passed her summer Greek course and in the fall began her senior year. She was amazed to learn that she and Jim had nearly identical class schedules: three Greek classes (Thucydides, Herodotus, and the Septuagint) and ancient Greek. Soon she and Jim were studying Greek together almost every night.

As Christmas approached, Betty felt attracted to Jim Elliot. Her brother Dave had invited Jim home to New Jersey for the holidays. Betty wondered how she would feel when Jim was introduced to the rest of her family. Would he fit in with the very organized daily routines at home? What would her parents and siblings think of him? And then she wondered why she even cared. After all, Jim was just another study mate, someone she never expected to see again after she graduated and had gone off to Africa or the South Seas. Or was he? Because Betty had no way of knowing whether he would ever reappear in her life, the thought of spending Christmas with her family and Jim both thrilled and terrified her.

Christmas with Jim was an eye-opening experience for Betty. Jim was well up to the task of fitting in with the formal, structured routine of the Howard family. And he really did know the Bible better than any of her brothers or her sister. But most astonishing of all, Jim could recite more hymns and poems than all of them put together. Betty found herself marveling at Jim. One minute he was reciting the entire twenty-one stanzas of the hymn *The Sands of Time Are Sinking,* and the next minute he was quoting Amy Carmichael, Betty's favorite author.

At home in Moorestown, Betty visited old friends in New Jersey and Philadelphia and helped her mother around the house. Meanwhile, Jim shoveled snow from the front driveway and fixed several plumbing problems in the house. At night after everyone else had gone to bed, Betty and Jim would often sit and talk for an hour or longer. They had so much in common: they were both studying Greek, they both wanted to be missionaries, and they both loved learning about the Bible and reading about great saints like Amy Carmichael and Hudson Taylor. But sometimes as they talked, Betty wondered whether there wasn't a hint of something else in their conversations. Was something deeper going on? She could not be sure.

In January, Betty, Dave, and Jim rode the train back to Wheaton. This was Betty's last semester at college, and she had a lot of work to do.

It was four months later, at the end of April, before Jim asked Betty out on a date. After Greek class one afternoon, Jim told Betty that he was off to a missionary meeting at Moody Church in Chicago and wanted to know whether Betty would like to go with him to the event.

Betty was happy to be asked. She had been thinking of attending the meeting anyway, since the guest speaker was one of the daughters of C. T. Studd, a brave and dedicated early missionary to Africa. And

C. T. Studd's daughter did not disappoint. Her talk was riveting, especially when she described her father's death. Her father lived in a tiny hut with very few possessions. He looked around and said, "I wish I had something to leave to each of you, but I gave it all to Jesus long ago."

The talk fired up Jim, who talked about the sacrifices of the soul on their trip back to Wheaton College. When she thought about it later that night, Betty had to concede that it had not been a romantic date. And she was not surprised when Jim did not ask her out again.

The end of the school year loomed ahead, and on Memorial Day the Foreign Missions Fellowship at Wheaton College met for the last time that semester. The group gathered for breakfast outside at a place called the Lagoon. It felt strange to Betty to be sitting around chatting with people she had come to know and love over the past four years, knowing that they were about to be scattered to the four winds. One old roommate was off to Africa as a missionary, another to medical school, and several others to various missionary training programs. Although Betty felt called to the mission field as a Bible translator, she was not sure just how God was going to lead her there.

When the breakfast meeting was over, a group of the regular attendees stayed to clean up. Betty volunteered to help and noted that Jim did also. Betty was stuffing the last few pieces of trash into a can when Jim came bounding up to her. "Walk you back to your dorm?" he said.

Betty nodded. She needed to get back, as she had packing to do in anticipation of graduating and leaving Wheaton College behind. The two of them walked in silence for a quarter of a mile, and then Jim turned to Betty and touched her arm. "We have to get squared away how we feel about each other," he said.

Betty stared at him. "Feel about each other. You mean…" she said slowly, trying to create a little time to think things through. Had she interpreted Jim's words correctly? Did he have feelings for her, and did he assume that she had some for him? Betty frowned. She thought she'd done a great job of hiding her feelings for Jim.

"Come on, Betty," Jim said impatiently, as if she were playing a game with him. "Don't tell me you didn't know I was in love with you."

"I had no idea," Betty stammered.

"Really?" Jim looked incredulous. He detailed all the times they had studied together, all the times he had stopped to talk with her after class, the long talks over Christmas, and the conversation on the train coming back to campus from New Jersey.

"I guess I did notice that you spent a lot of time with me," Betty said. "But I told myself you were just being a Christian brother, that you couldn't possibly be interested in me, much less in love with me!"

"I don't think we should go back yet," Jim said. "How about we go back to the Lagoon and do some serious talking."

And serious talking it was. Betty was reeling from the fact that Jim said he loved her, and she was

equally floored by his admission that God was calling him to the life of a single missionary.

As they talked, it seemed that they were both
wrestling with the same problem: was married life
for either of them, or was God requiring them to be
single and serve Him that way?

Betty's mind raced to the instructions that she
had often heard her father give to her brothers: "Son,
never tell a woman that you love her unless you ask
to marry her in the next sentence." For whatever reason, Betty mused, Jim did not appear to have gotten
that message from his own father. And now where
would it lead them?

Jim and Betty agreed they loved each other. They
also agreed that they felt God was calling them to be
single missionaries.

That night, as Betty tried to pray about the matter, she felt elation one moment and despair the next.
Why was it so difficult to figure out the right thing to
do? Why would God let her love someone—someone
as godly as Jim Elliot—and then not lead them both
to get married soon?

Betty's parents asked her the same thing when
they came for graduation. Family finances were low,
and her mother had had to sell a silver rose bowl—
a Gillingham family heirloom—for travel expenses
to Wheaton. When they arrived, Betty's parents
expressed their concerns about Betty and Jim. "God
is not the author of confusion," Philip Howard said to
his daughter. "Keep praying. God will make it clear
what you are to do next."

But clarity did not come quickly.

Chapter 7

Turmoil

Steam billowed out from under the engine of the *Texas Chief.* Betty and Jim clasped hands. She waited for him to crush her in an embrace, to say they would get married soon, that they would never have to say goodbye again, but it did not happen. Instead Jim smiled at Betty, squeezed her hand, and let it go.

Betty turned, lifted her suitcase, walked the length of the Chicago train station platform, and climbed aboard the train. Tears streamed down her face as she found a seat, stowed her bag, and sat down. She stared out the window thinking, *One more train ride. One more time I have to trust God that He knows what He is doing—that He sees the full picture, even though I don't.*

Betty tried to center her thoughts on God's will, but it was difficult. As the *Texas Chief* rolled by each station—Springfield, Kansas City, Wichita—her heart ached for Jim, and her thoughts were filled with him. What was he doing right now? Would he write to her this summer? Should she plan to visit him at Wheaton College next year, or would she wait for him to invite her? What had he meant by that final squeeze of her hand? Had he meant anything?

As she often did, Betty quietly recited a poem to help her make sense of her feelings. The poem was by Alice Meynell:

Let this goodbye of ours, this last goodbye
Be still and splendid like a forest tree...
Let there be one grand look within our eyes,
Built of the wonderment of the past years,
Too vast a thing of beauty to be lost
In quivering lips and burning floods of tears.

The poem did not comfort her much. Too many questions remained. Would this be their last goodbye? Was their love for each other something too beautiful to be lost? Or was it something God wanted Betty to sacrifice to her larger goal of following Him? Betty did not know, and she realized that was the way it was going to have to be until further notice from Jim.

Red-eyed and exhausted, Betty disembarked the train in Norman, Oklahoma. A pickup truck was waiting at the station to take her to the University of Oklahoma, where she would stay for the summer.

The next morning classes began, and Betty recognized a handful of students from Wheaton College among the other students. Betty was excited to be a part of the Summer Institute of Linguistics, or SIL, as everyone called it. She was there to learn cutting-edge linguistic techniques that would enable her to go to a tribal group, learn all there was to know about their language—from speaking it to how the grammar and syntax held together—and then begin translating portions of Scripture into that language. Cameron Townsend and L. L. Legters had started the Summer Institute of Linguistics in 1934. L. L. Legters had stayed at the Howard house on various occasions, and Betty fondly remembered him.

SIL estimated that there were at least a thousand unwritten languages in the world, but as Betty soon learned, that number was increasing almost daily as new languages were discovered. The whole purpose of SIL was to train linguists who could write down these languages so that Bible translation could begin. Betty listened carefully to lectures about the structure of the languages and how to go about the initial task of learning them. But the program was not just classroom bound. The participants in the institute had fieldwork to do. Six or seven of the students were assigned to an Indian, referred to as an informant, who spoke a language that the students did not know. It was the students' job to learn the language, write it down, and then translate something into that language. The program was challenging for Betty but also fulfilling as she learned important principles of linguistics—principles she hoped to one day put to work in Africa.

In the evening the students had time off, and during this time Betty often chose to take walks alone. The huge football stadium was one of her favorite destinations. She would climb up to the top row of bleachers, often just in time to catch a spectacular sunset. Most of the time, however, it was not the sunset but thoughts of Jim Elliot that captured her attention. Jim invaded all aspects of her life. When she tried to pray, she ended up praying for Jim; when she studied morphology or syntax or phonetics, her mind was cast back to the study hall at Wheaton College with her and Jim sitting elbow to elbow learning Greek.

Each day Betty secretly hoped for some sign from Jim—a letter, a postcard, even a phone call—but none ever came. She wrote in her journal, "Silence begins to drag on my soul. It is a kind of waiting which hears no voice, no footstep, sees no sign. I feel that I could wait ten years, if it were not for this waiting, this silence."

The eleven-week Summer Institute of Linguistics came to an end, but Betty decided to continue with her linguistic studies. She enrolled in the Prairie Bible Institute in Alberta, Canada, the same institution her brother Phil had attended for high school.

Even so, Betty was shocked when she saw the place. It had an old wooden farmhouse, some outbuildings, and a few newer buildings, low-slung and dark. It was more barren and remote than Phil had described. She hated to think how sparse the land-scape would be in winter under three feet of snow.

Betty was used to the strictures of boarding school and the social rules at Wheaton College, but nothing compared to the discipline required to stay at the Prairie Bible Institute. On the day she arrived, Betty was handed a thirty-two-page rule book. "Learn them all," the admissions officer told her. "We expect all sixteen hundred students to be compliant with them tomorrow morning."

As soon as Betty was shown her dorm room, she unpacked her few belongings and flipped open the rule book. There were rules for everything: the sleeves on girls' dresses and blouses had to extend at least three inches below the elbow, and skirt hems were to be no more than an inch off the floor when kneeling. Girls were to have long hair or, if they had just enrolled, commit themselves to growing their hair long. All meal and chapel times were to be strictly adhered to.

The book had a whole section titled "Water Usage." The school was seven miles from the nearest water supply, and all of the water had to be trucked in. There was a central water spigot, and at certain times a student could collect a bucket of water for his or her room. A second bucket was to be used for the collection of used water, which had another complicated set of instructions as to how and where it was to be disposed of.

As Betty read through all the rules relating to "boys and girls," she could hardly believe what she was reading. Students were allowed to walk off campus and onto the prairie on Sunday afternoons, but when they did, girls were to head north while the boys went south. Outside of school hours, boys and girls were forbidden to talk to each other.

At twenty-one years of age, Betty felt these rules were excessive. Even at Hampden DuBose Academy in Orlando, boys and girls worked side by side, and at Wheaton College she and Jim had studied together. But no such activities would be tolerated at the Prairie Bible Institute. However, Betty soon decided that it didn't really matter whether she was forbidden to talk to boys. The only boy she wanted to talk to was Jim Elliot, and he wasn't there.

Betty settled into life and study at the Prairie Bible Institute and tried to live by all of the rules, though she was lonely and homesick much of the time. She prayed for help, and it came in the form of a small, plump Scottish woman who knocked on Betty's door one Saturday morning. "Are you Betty Howard?" the woman asked.

"Yes," Betty said.

"Well, then, Betty dear," the woman said in a strong Scottish brogue, "you don't know me, but I have been praying for you since you got here. I thought perhaps it was time we got to know each other. Would you care to come down to my apartment? I'm about to make a pot of tea."

Betty followed the woman—who said her name was Mrs. Cunningham—to her basement apartment, where she was welcomed into a tiny living room.

"Now you just sit down right there, lass," Mrs. Cunningham said, pointing to a well-worn tapestry chair, "and I'll bring tea and scones. You do like scones and jam, don't you?"

Betty smiled and nodded. It felt good to be in a cozy home.

As she sipped the tea that was poured for her from a steaming teapot, Betty found herself pouring her heart out to Mrs. Cunningham. She told her about how she loved Jim Elliot and he loved her, but that they were putting God first and did not even know whether they were supposed to be on the mission field together or to be living single lives. Betty confided that she felt called to mission work in Africa, while Jim seemed certain that he would be going to South America.

Mrs. Cunningham nodded, and Betty could see compassion in the woman's bright blue eyes.

"It seems to me that we need prayer," Mrs. Cunningham said when Betty had finished. "Let's go to the Lord." With that she opened her Bible and read Romans 15, verse 13: "'May the God of hope fill you with all joy and peace in believing.' That's what's important, Betty," she said, her eyes shining. "You can have peace anytime, anywhere, dear, if you allow God to fill you with the joy of believing in Him and the immense wonder of being His child. Let's pray."

The two women sat in silence a minute or so, and then Mrs. Cunningham prayed. Betty left the apartment feeling unburdened, buoyed with the knowledge that she had a prayer partner and a friend.

Only days later Betty heard a set of footsteps outside her door. It was the mail delivery. The footsteps stopped, and she heard the sound of a letter being slipped under the door. Betty's heart skipped a beat. Was it a letter from Jim Elliot at last? Betty jumped up to get the letter. Sure enough, there was an envelope with Jim's distinctive handwriting on it. Her hands shook as she picked up the envelope, tore it open, and began to read:

Beloved,
...I wish I had a "feel-o-meter" to transcribe what has been going on inside for the last few days. It began with that word I think I spoke to you of when we were together in the chapel that last morning; trembling.

Betty read on. Jim wrote how he trembled at the thought that he had made her life more difficult by declaring his love for her, trembled at the thought that he might have made it more difficult to understand what God's will was for her, and trembled at the thought that he might find himself loving her more than he loved God and willing to compromise God's work for his own desires.

When she had read the letter through twice, Betty sat down to think about it. She was glad Jim had written, but in many ways his words did not clarify anything or settle her soul. But, Betty mused, at least she had Mrs. Cunningham to pray with about the matter.

Fall gave way to a harsh Canadian winter—the harshest winter in years. With limited heating in the buildings, Betty imagined that this was what it must be like staying in Gale Cottage in New Hampshire in winter. She piled on layers of warm clothes and sometimes didn't even take them off to sleep. On most mornings the top several inches of the water in the bucket in her room was frozen solid.

Given their remote location and the harsh winter, most of the students did not go home for Christmas, and Betty was no exception. Christmas Day was bitter cold—23 degrees below zero. Betty spent Christmas morning doing laundry and thinking about the wonderful times she'd had at Christmas as a child. It was the simple things she remembered most: the single green candlestick with holly berries on it that was placed in the front window; the stockings that hung from the end of the bed, filled mysteriously in the night with toothpaste, chewing gum, Cashmere Bouquet talcum powder, pencils, paper, and erasers; and Aunt Alice and Aunt Anne arriving for a delicious Christmas dinner of turkey, mashed potatoes, peas, pumpkin pie, and fruit mince pies. As Betty hung her wet clothes over the radiator to dry, she wondered what her parents were doing this Christmas and, more important, where in the world she would be this time next year. She wondered whether this would be her last Christmas in North America. A year from now, might she be living in a grass hut in the African jungle?

Chapter 8

A Certain Calling

Betty looked forward to Jim's letters, which arrived at six-week intervals. Sometimes in his letters Jim sounded hopeful that they would spend their lives together, and at other times his words were more guarded. At times his message was clear, and at other times Betty was confused by his words. However, it was a letter from Jim's mother that sent Betty into a tailspin.

As the school year at Prairie Bible Institute was ending, Betty received a letter from Jim's mother suggesting that she make a detour to the Elliots' home in Portland, Oregon, on her way back to New Jersey for the summer. Betty agonized endlessly in her diary about the letter. Would it be too forward of her to visit Jim's house when he had not invited her? Had Jim's mother discussed with him the invitation to come and visit? Would Jim be glad to see her, or did he want to focus solely on preparing for the mission field as a single man?

Betty tormented herself with such questions until she prayed about the situation with Mrs. Cunningham. After she had prayed, she felt that it was all right for her to accept the invitation. She bought a Greyhound bus ticket and braced herself for the six-hundred-mile journey to Portland.

Betty was a ball of nerves all the way to Oregon. She tried reading a book to take her mind off arriving at her destination, but that didn't help much. For a good part of the journey, she sat next to a sailor. Betty did not realize how obvious her nervousness was until the sailor said to her, "I have never seen a person sit so still. You haven't moved an inch the whole trip. Are you nervous or scared or something?"

Betty did not answer his question.

The bus rumbled into the bus station in Portland, where Jim was waiting for her, looking confident and full of life as usual. On the way to the Elliot home, Jim did most of the talking. He told Betty all about his last year at Wheaton College and what he had been able to accomplish as president of the Foreign Missions Fellowship. But when Betty pressed him about what he was going to do next, Jim was vague. He told her that he was convinced he would be a missionary somewhere in South America someday, and that all he felt sure about right now was that he should stay with his parents in Oregon and help his brother Bob build a house.

Soon they were driving up to the family home at 7272 Southeast Thorburn Street. The house was a two-story weatherboard structure set on the gently sloping side of Mount Tabor. Jim had two older brothers, Bert and Bob, and a younger sister, Jane, along with numerous relatives, most of whom were members of the Plymouth Brethren denomination. Together the family formed a large tangle of aunts, uncles, cousins, and second cousins.

Chapel meetings, as the Brethren referred to their services, and especially the Labor Day Conference, were like huge family reunions, with everyone hugging and kissing and talking over each other. It was nothing like the reserved, disciplined family life that Betty was used to, and she struggled to cope and fit in with the Elliots. Jim's reaction didn't help either. He swore that he was more devoted to Betty than ever but that he had no idea what their future together might look like.

The days in Portland that Betty truly enjoyed were those when she had Jim all to herself. The two of them went canoeing, hiked on the side of Mt. Hood, swam, and explored a remote seaside cove. It was the first time Betty had experienced the Pacific Ocean, and she loved the way the waves broke on the rugged Oregon coast and the wisps of fog that drifted in from the gray sea.

As the week in Portland wore on, however, Betty realized that she was not making a good impression on Jim's parents, who complained to Jim that they thought she was unfriendly. Of course, this mortified Betty. Didn't they realize that she was too nervous and too stressed to think about small talk with the family?

Betty was both relieved and distraught when it came time to leave Jim in Portland. She had hoped he would have a green light on their relationship. The deserted cove would have been an ideal place to propose marriage to her, but Jim had remained silent. And now they faced another year apart. After spending time in New Jersey with her parents, Betty intended to head back to Alberta, to a small rural town called Patience, where she would be working with the Canadian Sunday School Mission, helping to bring the gospel to a largely unevangelized community.

As she left Portland, Oregon, behind, Betty thought about when she would see Jim again. It would be next summer in Wheaton at her brother Dave's wedding. Dave had proposed to a fellow Wheaton graduate named Phyllis Gibson and had asked Jim to be his best man. Betty was to be one of the bridesmaids.

As the summer of 1950 approached, Betty found herself looking forward to her brother's wedding. She could not help comparing Dave and Phyllis's relationship to her and Jim's relationship. Both couples had known each other for about the same length of time, but Dave and Phyllis had an uncomplicated courtship: they had fallen in love, sought God's and their parents' blessings, and planned a wedding.

How Betty wished it had been that easy for her and Jim.

Yet sometimes things did seem to be moving forward in their relationship. Jim had written to tell Betty that he would not consider marriage until he was settled in a missionary location, and now Jim's letters indicated that he was seriously praying about becoming a missionary to Ecuador. Betty waited eagerly for each new letter. Jim told how his brother Bert, a missionary in Peru, had forwarded a letter to him from Dr. Wilfred Tidmarsh, an English missionary who worked with the Quichua Indians in Ecuador. In the letter Dr. Tidmarsh said his wife had medical problems, which meant that the couple had to leave their new work among the Quichua in a remote jungle location called Shandia. Dr. Tidmarsh concluded the letter by asking Bert if he could forward it to anyone who might be interested in taking over the missionary work at Shandia. Jim confided to Betty that he was very interested in taking over the work and that he had written a letter explaining this to Dr. Tidmarsh but had not yet sent it. He was not sure enough that this was God's will for him, and he did not want to do anything that might displease God.

In July, Betty headed for Wheaton, Illinois, for Dave and Phyllis's wedding. She enjoyed the festivities and being with her family again, but mostly she enjoyed seeing Jim. That summer Jim was attending the Summer Institute of Linguistics in Oklahoma and had taken time off to drive up to the wedding. Yet as she and Jim spent time together, Betty was aware that nothing had changed in the status of their relationship. She still did not know what to do next. While she believed God was calling her to the mission field, she had no clear guidance as to where that might be. Her only option was to wait and pray about the matter.

Meanwhile, Dr. Pierre DuBose from the Hampden DuBose Academy in Orlando had written to ask Betty if she would come and teach public speaking at the school for a semester. Betty accepted the offer and once more found herself on a train headed south. Since her graduation, the Hampden DuBose Academy had relocated to a tiny town called Zellwood, about twenty miles northwest of Orlando and the original school that Betty had attended.

Betty found the new school location breathtaking. It consisted of an old mansion set on a hundred acres of woods and lakes. The place had once been the hunting lodge of a steel magnate named James Laughlin. The mansion had thirteen bedrooms and seven bathrooms and formal English gardens, which enchanted Betty. There was even a swimming pool in the basement and an elaborate system of fans to bring cool air up to the bedrooms. Betty found it interesting to see from a teacher's perspective how the school she had attended was run. Her roommate was Miss Andy, whom she now called Jane. Jane was constantly in motion, writing notes to parents, grading papers, supervising the kitchen, organizing outings, and chauffeuring children to and from the bus station. Betty had had no idea when she was a student at the academy just how much work went on behind the scenes.

After the semester, and with new admiration for the teachers at the Hampden DuBose Academy, Betty left Zellwood and headed home to New Jersey to pray seriously about her future. She was now twenty-four years old, and she felt it was time to make some big decisions.

Betty's focus for missionary service had always been Africa or the islands of the South Pacific. But as she continued to pray, asking God to reveal to her clearly where it was that He wanted her to go, Betty met Catherine Morgan. Catherine and her husband had been Plymouth Brethren missionaries in Bogotá, Colombia, for many years, but when her husband got sick, they had come back to New York so that he could receive proper medical treatment. Despite the treatment, her husband had died. And now Catherine was living in New York, working for a missionary magazine, and planning to return to Colombia and continue her work there.

Betty found herself drawn to Catherine, and soon the two women became good friends. Whenever they got together to talk, Catherine would challenge Betty about the focus of where she should be a missionary. She urged Betty to consider going to South America, perhaps to Colombia or to next-door Ecuador, where there was a growing need for missionaries.

At first Betty resisted Catherine's suggestion. In her mind South America was much too close to the

United States. She had imagined herself going to the other side of the world to serve as a missionary, not to South America. Yet as she and Catherine continued to talk and as she prayed about the situation, Betty began to feel that perhaps South America was where God was leading her after all.

Once Betty was certain that South America was where God wanted her as a missionary, Catherine suggested she move to New York to begin her training. She knew of a small Spanish-speaking Puerto Rican church in Brooklyn, New York, that would be willing to have Betty come and live in the tiny walk-up apartment they kept for visiting missionaries. Catherine explained that this would be a great opportunity for Betty to begin learning Spanish before setting out for South America.

Betty Howard thus found herself living on the fifth floor of a rundown tenement building in Brooklyn. The building had no elevator and only intermittent hot water and heat. But those were not the biggest problems; that "honor" belonged to the rats! The rats were enormous—large enough to turn over a trash can and rummage through its contents—and they roamed freely about the building. Betty made sure to make lots of noise when entering or leaving the apartment, giving the rats ample warning to get out of her way. Of course, she had no plan of attack if she were ever to corner one of the rats by accident. And as she climbed up and down the stairs each day, she tried to ignore the aromas of strange food cooking that floated out from other apartments.

Yes, the place was smelly and dark and rat-infested, and the Spanish lessons with the church pastor were not as frequent as Betty had hoped they would be, but she thanked God for bringing her to Brooklyn. It was a stepping-stone in a definite direction, and that was something she was very glad about. For the first time in a long time, Betty had clarity about her future. She had prayed earnestly about going to Africa and even to the South Pacific, but God had set her firmly on a path to South America. As she prayed for Him to show her where in South America, she felt the answer was Ecuador—with or without Jim Elliot.

Shortly afterward, Dorothy Jones, a young woman from Texas whom Betty had met at the Summer Institute of Linguistics in Oklahoma, came to live with her in the apartment in Brooklyn. Dorothy also felt called to mission service in Ecuador, and now the two women made preparations to go there together.

Letters continued to flow between Jim and Betty. Jim had finally sent the letter he had written to Dr. Tidmarsh in Ecuador, and now, independent of each other, the two of them were plotting their separate courses to get to the tiny South American country.

Like Dorothy Jones, Betty had been accepted for missionary service by the Plymouth Brethren mission agency Christian Missions in Many Lands, and the plan was for the two of them to travel to Quito, the capital of Ecuador, and study Spanish there together before being assigned to work with an indigenous group who needed the Bible translated into their own language.

Meanwhile, Jim and a fellow student from Wheaton College, Pete Fleming, were making final preparations for their departure for Ecuador. The letters back and forth between Jim and Dr. Tidmarsh had convinced Jim that he was on the right track. On February 2, 1952, Jim called Betty on the telephone to say goodbye. It was the first time the two of them had ever spoken long-distance. Because it was a very expensive call, they talked only briefly. Jim was excited about leaving, and he expected that they would meet up again in Quito if Betty and Dorothy went ahead with their plans.

As far as Betty Howard was concerned, there was no "if" about it. Betty was now certain of her calling and willing and ready to begin Bible translation work somewhere in Ecuador. It was merely a matter of where and when.

Ecuador

B etty Howard almost had to pinch herself as she looked over the ship's railing. The ship was sailing up the Guayas River toward Guayaquil, Ecuador. It had set sail from New York ten days before, heading south and then west across the Caribbean and on through the Panama Canal to the Pacific Ocean. It had then followed the west coast of South America and was now approaching its destination.

Guayaquil looked completely different from the huge, bustling city of New York. It had no tall skyscrapers. The city consisted of wooden buildings spread along the western bank of the Guayas River. But while Guayaquil, the largest city in Ecuador, looked completely different from New York, it too was a city of bustle and business. It was the main port

for the country, and the Guayas River was studded
with all manner of vessels, from ships to small dugout canoes loaded down with bunches of bananas.
And on land, people seemed to be milling around
everywhere. The city was also hot and humid and
reminded Betty of the climate in Orlando, Florida.

"Can you believe it?" Dorothy said. "April 12, 1952,
the day we finally begin our missionary work!" She
grinned with excitement as their vessel approached
the dock.

Once ashore, Betty and Dorothy were met by a
Plymouth Brethren couple who helped them get their
belongings through customs and then took them to
their home. Betty hardly slept that night as she contemplated what lay ahead the next day—a flight
over the spine of the spectacular Andes Mountains to
Quito. She had never been in an airplane before and
didn't quite know what to expect, and she had read
several travel accounts that touted the flight to Quito
as spectacular.

Betty was not disappointed by the trip. Despite
some apprehension as the plane took off from the
airport in Guayaquil, she soon relaxed. Flying, she
decided, was indeed the way to travel. As the airplane continued to climb and leave the Pacific coast
of Ecuador behind, the Andes came into view. The
mountain range was more massive than Betty could
have imagined. From the air the mountains seemed
to go on forever, as high, barren, rocky peaks, clad
in blankets of ice and snow, reached toward the sky.
Finally the plane began to circle and descend. Below

her, Betty could see Quito, nestled at ninety-three hundred feet above sea level in a large valley surrounded by snowy mountain peaks. The accounts of flying into Quito that Betty had read were right—the vista spread below the airplane was spectacular.

The plane landed and taxied to a standstill on the tarmac at the Quito airport. As Betty and Dorothy deplaned, a group of missionaries met them. The group included Jim Elliot and Pete Fleming. Betty, of course, was delighted to see Jim, and after welcoming her to Quito, Jim explained that he and Pete were staying at the home of a local doctor while they learned and became fluent in Spanish. Betty and Dorothy would be staying in a house across the street from Jim and Pete.

Life in Quito fell into an easy pattern for Betty. As young missionary trainees, Betty and Dorothy, along with Jim and Pete, studied Spanish together each morning and then had their midday meal. Sometimes in the afternoon, Dr. Wilfred Tidmarsh, the senior Plymouth Brethren missionary in Ecuador, gave lectures on relevant topics related to living and working in the country. On their first day together, Dr. Tidmarsh told Betty a little about his background. He explained that he had a PhD in geology and had been a university professor in England. In his spare time he loved to read about strange and remote places, and he was especially drawn to Ecuador. He wondered why the place was among the most backward countries on earth and why the gospel had not taken a stronger hold there.

Eventually, Dr. Tidmarsh told Betty, he came to believe that God was calling him and his wife, Gwen, to work in Ecuador. They had sold their belongings, and he had enrolled in a one-year emergency medical course. When he had completed the course, he was accepted as a missionary in Ecuador to the Quichua Indians. For the past thirteen years the Tidmarshes had been living and working among the Quichua. Like Betty, Dr. Tidmarsh had a flare for languages and had compiled the most complete Quichua dictionary available. But the work had taken its toll. Dr. Tidmarsh was gaunt and pale from bouts of malaria, yet he exuded a cheerfulness that Betty prayed she could match when her time finally came to go and work among one of Ecuador's indigenous Indian groups.

Every day was a wonderful new adventure for Betty, and the time was made all the more magical by having Jim at her side. Betty and Jim often planned adventures together. They liked to take the bus sixteen miles north to La Mitad del Mundo, where the equator ran right through the middle of town. They would stroll through the Mercado de Santa Clara, stopping to smell the huge bunches of freshly cut flowers for sale at the market and admire the Indian weaving and baskets. One day Betty and Jim and a group of other trainee missionaries climbed Mount Pichincha. And on Ecuador's Labor Day holiday, Jim took Betty to a bullfight. It was the first bullfight either of them had been to, and Betty did not know quite what to expect.

The bullring was packed to capacity with excited people who stood and cheered when the matador entered the ring. The matador was dressed in an elaborately decorated suit, with long white stockings to just below his knees and shiny black shoes. He acknowledged the cheers of the crowd and then took his place in the center of the ring. Moments later a large black bull raced into the ring and headed straight for the matador, who held out his cape. At the last moment the matador stepped sideways and turned as the charging bull raced by him only inches away.

Back and forth the bull and the matador went, and Jim told Betty that the matador's movements were almost like ballet. Betty had to agree. There was a certain graceful, dancelike fluidness to the way the matador moved to avoid being gored by the bull. But as the bull began to tire, the illusion of ballet quickly came to an end as Betty watched the matador thrust a sword through the majestic animal. Betty turned away as the crowd stood to their feet cheering and clapping. Although bullfighting was not something Betty cared to see again, she had to admit that it had been an interesting cross-cultural experience.

Jim and Pete were two months ahead of Betty and Dorothy in their Spanish language studies. By late spring Dr. Tidmarsh was preparing the two young men for the next stage of their mission—moving into a jungle station in the Oriente, as the eastern Amazon Basin of Ecuador was called. As planned, the place they were going to was Shandia, the mission station Dr. Tidmarsh had established and manned for five years before reluctantly relinquishing the post because of his wife's ill health and moving to Quito.

Jim explained to Betty that Shandia was located in the jungle alongside the Atun Yaku River. While living there, Dr. Tidmarsh had built a large hut on piles. The hut had a thatched roof, and Dr. Tidmarsh thought they would have to do a lot of repair work to make it habitable again. The house had been empty since he and his wife left Shandia, and everything deteriorated quickly in the jungle.

Betty could see how excited Jim was to be moving into the jungle after six months in Quito. Jim was eager to learn the Quichua language and start his evangelistic work.

During this time, Jim told Betty about another group of Indians who lived in the jungle of the Oriente not too far from Shandia. These Indians were called the Aucas and were a Stone Age tribe that spoke their own language and kept themselves isolated from other tribes and outsiders. They had a reputation for being the most violent tribe in the Oriente. People said that they would kill a man or woman with their spears for no apparent reason. Jim told Betty this was probably true. The Aucas had speared to death a number of men working in the jungle for the Shell Oil Company. Jim told Betty that although he could not explain it, he felt strangely drawn to the challenge of one day sharing the gospel with this unreached tribe of Indians. Because of this, he had made it a point to gather information on them, though there was not much to be had. Few people who met the Aucas lived to tell about it.

Before long it was time for Jim and Pete to begin their new venture in Shandia. Betty noticed that Jim put off saying goodbye as long as he could. But the reality that the two of them were going their separate ways set in. When they finally said their farewells, Jim apologized because although he professed his love for Betty, he did not feel God leading him to marry. He said that there was simply too much work for a single man to do in Ecuador. Of course, Betty was disappointed at his explanation, yet she had to admit she was still struggling with whether she also should be married or remain a single missionary. Because there was a lot of work for a single woman missionary to do in Ecuador, she turned her focus to her future in the country.

Dr. Tidmarsh urged Betty and Dorothy to pray about where they should go. He told them about two young English women, Doreen Clifford and Barbara Edwards, who were struggling to hold down the fort, as he put it, running a tiny school and mission outpost among the Colorado Indians in San Miguel de los Colorados. This was forty-five miles west of Quito on the broad, jungle-covered coastal plain between the Andes Mountains and the Pacific Ocean. He suggested that the two of them consider going there for a period of time to help the two English missionary women with their work among the Colorado Indians. The Colorados, Dr. Tidmarsh explained, were one of nine indigenous tribes in Ecuador, and their language had never been written down. As a result, no Bibles or other gospel materials existed in their language.

Betty's heart soared as she contemplated joining Doreen and Barbara in San Miguel. Because neither of these two missionaries was a linguist, the job of learning the language of the Colorados and reducing it to a written vocabulary would fall to Betty and Dorothy. Betty was particularly excited about the opportunity to be the first to record the Colorados' language and then, she hoped, work to translate the Bible into their language for them.

In early September 1952, the day arrived for Betty and Dorothy to leave for San Miguel de los Colorados. Betty packed file boxes and cards, spare pens and bottles of ink, dictionaries and Bibles—tools that she would need to help in the work of reducing the Colorados' language to written form. Very early one morning an old pickup truck pulled up outside the house where they were staying in Quito. The man driving the pickup was an American missionary, whom everyone simply called E.T. He and his wife and children lived and worked among the Colorados at Santo Domingo, which was on the way to San Miguel. The pickup truck was loaded high with supplies, leaving the tailgate as the only place for Betty and Dorothy to sit. The women took their positions, their hands gripping the side of the truck.

First the pickup climbed up and out of the valley in which Quito was nestled and headed for the village of San Juan, located at an altitude of eleven thousand feet. San Juan marked the start of the road that would take them down the western slope of the Andes onto the coastal plain. However, this road was so narrow and winding that vehicles could travel on it only in one direction at a time. A chain was stretched across the road and was dropped only at nine in the morning and two in the afternoon for vehicles headed west. Unfortunately, despite their early start, they managed to miss the nine o'clock dropping of the chain and were forced to wait until two o'clock that afternoon. The wait was not at all comfortable, as a misty rain settled over the area. Betty passed the time eating ears of freshly boiled sweet corn and fried potatoes, which she bought at the small make-shift store beside the road.

Finally the two o'clock chain was dropped, and off they went. E.T. explained that a man would count the number of vehicles headed down the road before putting the chain back up. He would then radio that number to a man at the chain at the other end of the road. When that number of vehicles had passed through the chain at the other end, vehicles would be allowed to start traveling the road in the opposite direction.

The road down the Andes was more narrow, winding, precarious, and bumpy than Betty could have imagined. Betty and Dorothy balanced on the tailgate, often staring over the edge of the road and straight down hundreds or even thousands of feet to the bottom of a ravine. Along the way were many rivers and streams to cross. Some had rickety bridges over them, but many didn't, causing E.T. to ford them, splashing water on Betty and Dorothy.

It was nearly midnight when E.T. finally pulled the pickup truck to a halt. "We're home," he called out as he cut the engine.

After fifteen hours of sitting and holding the side of the pickup so tightly that her knuckles were white and her bottom was numb, Betty slid off the tailgate and gingerly stood up. Every bone in her body ached as she stumbled into the tiny, blackened shanty.

After all she had been through, Betty would have loved a strong cup of coffee in clean, comfortable surroundings, but it was not to be. She was not sure which hit her first, the putrid stench of the field beside the house that seemed to serve as a public latrine or the damp smell of the house's moldy walls. And it wasn't just the smell. The entire house had a depressing air about it. The room was filled with smoke, the few sticks of furniture in the room were old and rickety, and the curtains that partitioned off the room were filthy.

Even though it was midnight, four small children roamed the house, unable to sleep until their father returned. Their dirty, oversized clothes hung off them, and their skin was ingrained with dirt. Betty smiled and said hello, but none of them responded. She couldn't help but think of the training in manners the missionary children at the Hampden DuBose Academy received. What a contrast these four bedraggled urchins in front of her were to her fellow students at the academy.

Betty and Dorothy spent the weekend with E.T. and his wife, Vera. Betty counted every passing hour. She was appalled at the way E.T. and his family lived and was confused by her own reaction to the situation. Surely this family had given up everything, every semblance of civilization, to be missionaries. Wasn't that what she had been taught to do? Yet Betty wondered whether there was a place for beauty and light and cleanliness on the mission field. Was living in squalor part of taking up the cross to follow Christ? Betty sincerely hoped not, and it was with a mixture of relief and dread of what might lie ahead that she left Santo Domingo for San Miguel.

Chapter 10

San Miguel
de los Colorados

Betty breathed in the jungle smells. The air was more fragrant than she had imagined, with a wet earthy scent. And no wonder, she mused, as she looked down from her perch atop a pony. Everything she could see was green or brown and shiny. Moisture hung in the air like an invisible fog, coating everything with a fine layer of dampness. The trail they were following was thick with mud. In places the ponies were nearly up to their bellies in the boggy black sludge. Betty's legs were covered in mud, and she gave up worrying about her hair, which stuck to her forehead and neck. Her once-crisp cotton shirt was saturated and clung to her like a wet sponge.

None of this mattered to Betty, who continually reminded herself that she was actually sitting on a pony and riding through the Ecuadorian jungle on the way to decipher a never-before-written language. In front of her was a guide, and behind, Dorothy and two mules carrying their clothing and translation materials. She was living her dream!

As she rode along, Betty composed a letter home in her head. She would tell her father about the strange birdcalls she heard and give her aunt a description of the purple butterfly with the golden underside that had just fluttered by. Betty only hoped that she could describe it well enough.

After three bumpy hours on the trail, the ponies finally brought Betty and Dorothy to their destination—San Miguel de los Colorados. The place was just as E.T. had described it before they set out that morning—a clearing about four hundred feet across. About eight houses were nestled in the clearing, with two in particular standing out. The house on the left was a large barnlike structure made of split bamboo with a high-pitched thatched roof. E.T. had told Betty that the mission owned the home. In fact, he had built the place and lived in it himself. Next to this building Betty would find Doreen Clifford's home, a small two-story wood frame house with a neat fence around it.

Betty pulled on the reins and her pony headed toward the house. Before she had reached the house, a slender white woman came running out. She was about thirty years old, had wavy brown hair, and was wearing a floral dress. "Welcome, welcome!" she called out in a strong British accent. "Welcome to San Miguel-on-the-mud!"

Betty grinned. She already liked Doreen Clifford.

"We hoped you'd be here today," Doreen said. "I've delayed lunch just in case you made it today. Come on inside."

A second Englishwoman appeared. She was heavier set than Doreen, but she also had wavy brown hair and wore a floral patterned cotton dress. "Hi, I'm Barbara," she said. "I'll help the guide take care of the ponies."

Betty and Dorothy climbed down from the ponies. After a minute they regained their balance and then followed Doreen inside. Doreen gave the two new arrivals a quick tour of downstairs. A good part of the first floor was taken up with a medical clinic. The walls were lined with makeshift cupboards filled with bottles of pills, medical supplies, and instruments. A fully equipped dentist chair sat in one corner of the room. The rest of the downstairs was set up as a dormitory for girls attending the school run by the two Englishwomen.

Upstairs consisted of a large room screened on three sides. Handmade chairs and other pieces of furniture were spread about the room, and old kerosene boxes had been put to use as shelves. A long curtain partitioned off Doreen's bedroom from the rest of the room, and at the back of the room was a kitchen with a scrubbed board for a counter and more kerosene boxes to hold up the counter and serve as cupboard space. The kitchen contained several polished brass gasoline burners and a *fogón,* or wood-burning stove. Kitchen utensils hung neatly from a row of nails above the counter and stove.

Lunch was laid out on a green and orange plaid tablecloth that covered the dining table in the main room upstairs. Betty hungrily surveyed the food: spinach soup, rice, fried eggs, and tea made with scalded milk. It was a strange assortment of food, but after three hours on horseback on the muddy trail from Santo Domingo, Betty and Dorothy were grateful for it.

As the four women ate, they discussed plans for the future. Doreen took the lead, since she had been living there the longest. Betty soon learned that Doreen and Barbara had very different ideas of what the mission's work should be, and to a large extent the two women had gone their own ways.

Doreen, who had completed a course in missionary medicine in London, ran the downstairs clinic, while Barbara oversaw a small school for the children of white Ecuadorians and Colombians who lived in and around the area. Barbara told Betty she was interested in reaching out to the Colorado Indians but had not had much success to this point.

That left several openings for Betty and Dorothy to fill. Barbara desperately needed help with the school, and Dorothy was eager to be involved there. Betty asked about language studies. Had anyone tried learning the language of the Colorados? The answer was no. More disappointing news followed.

Doreen informed Betty that there were no Colorados living in San Miguel. In fact, Colorados did not live in settlements at all but were scattered throughout the jungle, isolated from each other and the world in general.

The good news was that the Colorados did know the mission existed, because it was en route to Santo Domingo, where they bought a few supplies. They would seek out the missionaries for help with difficult births, serious illnesses, and accidents. Other than that, Doreen told Betty, the Colorados were an independent lot who did not show much interest in the white man's ways. They were not afraid of or violent toward white people. For the most part, they just simply ignored them. Doreen told Betty she believed this was because they had lived in proximity to Europeans since the arrival of the Spanish conquistadors in Ecuador in 1531 and had decided long ago to stick to their own way of doing things. It made sense to Betty, who hoped to bring the gospel to these people but was faced with the stark challenge of how to do it without making them think it was a "white man's" message.

After lunch, Doreen took Betty and Dorothy on a tour of San Miguel. There wasn't really much to see, and the tour was over in a few minutes. The tour ended at Barbara Edwards' house, which was made of split bamboo and had a thatched roof. But the house was only a single story and sat precariously off the ground on bamboo poles. The women climbed the ladderlike staircase that led into the house.

Immediately Betty noticed the contrast between Barbara's and Doreen's houses. Barbara had a bed and a bench for sitting, and the only other furniture was the fogón in the small kitchen area. It appeared to Betty, judging by the interior of the house, that comfort was not particularly important to Barbara.

"And of course, that's where you two will live," Doreen announced, gesturing toward one of the big barnlike structures that Betty and Doreen had first seen upon their arrival.

Soon Betty and Dorothy were settled in, as much as a person with two saddlebags and a few boxes filled with belongings could be. The school occupied the first floor, while upstairs a large room ran the length of the building, with a kitchen at the back. Three bedrooms opened off the large room. Dorothy occupied the front bedroom; Marta, a nineteen-year-old Ecuadorian woman who taught in the school, occupied the middle bedroom; and Betty was in the back bedroom. Her bedroom was surprisingly large—too big to be made cozy with the few personal items she had brought with her.

As she arranged the small, red fireman's lantern she had brought from the United States and hung a plastic clothes bag to serve as a makeshift closet, Betty thought about what lay ahead for her. Her first task was to find an informant, someone who knew the Colorados' language well and was willing to sit with her and help her untangle its meaning.

Such a job was a labor of love for most informants. From her time attending the Summer Institute of

Linguistics in Oklahoma, Betty knew that the task was tedious. The informant would say a word over and over again while she would attempt to discern the particular sounds that made up the word and would then write them down. Sometimes she would have to sit for a long time and watch the informant's mouth and lips as he or she formed and repeated the word several times. This would give her some understanding of how the word should be said and a clearer understanding of its sound. The process could be long and torturous, but it was the first stage in getting a Bible in the language of the Colorados into their hands. First the language had to be understood and reduced to writing. Then the translation of the various books of the Bible into that language could begin. And just as important, the Colorados would have to be encouraged to learn to read their own language so that they could make use of the translated Bible.

Betty had a long and arduous task ahead of her. Often it took a team of people—like links in a chain—to accomplish the task. One person would begin the process, find a reliable informant, and begin writing the language down. A second person would then review and refine what the first person had accomplished, and so on, until a Bible had been translated and finally printed in the language.

Although she knew that she would be the first link in the chain, Betty did not know how long she was going to be stationed at San Miguel de los Colorados. She secretly hoped that Jim would propose to her and the two of them would marry and begin working together, though she had no idea whether or not this would happen. As she folded her clothes and stacked them in the kerosene box shelves in her bedroom, Betty resolved to leave that matter to God. For now she had a big enough challenge ahead of her.

And what a challenge finding an informant turned out to be. It was three days before Betty even saw her first Colorado Indian. She was hanging her bedsheets to dry on the clothesline at the back of the house when a Colorado man emerged from the jungle, riding a pony. The first thing she noticed about him was the tight red helmet he wore on his head. As the man rode closer, Betty could see that his body was painted a vivid red with black horizontal stripes beginning at his forehead and going all the way to his feet. The man also wore a black and white shirt that stopped just below his hips and was adorned with a brilliant yellow and turquoise scarf. The Colorado man rode over to Doreen's house, dismounted, and tied his pony to the fence. Betty quickly followed. When she got there, Doreen was talking to the man in Spanish. The man replied to her questions in halting Spanish. Betty surmised that he had come to get medicine from Doreen.

Betty studied the Indian up close as Doreen introduced her to him. She smiled, and he smiled back. His teeth, tongue, and lips were stained a bluish-black color. Betty's heart beat fast. Could this be the informant she had been praying for? She asked Doreen to offer him the job in Spanish, and Betty understood his reply. It was yes! Although he had to go home just then, he said he would surely return and help Betty next week.

As the Colorado mounted his pony and rode off back into the jungle, Betty asked Doreen about the man's helmet. "Why on earth does an Indian need to wear a helmet in the jungle?"

A bemused smile settled across Doreen's face. "A helmet?" she said. "Why, that's his hair!"

Betty felt her cheeks blush.

"Colorado men plaster their hair down with a mixture of Vaseline and achiote—a red dye they get from the seed pods of a certain tree. It may look like a helmet to the untrained eye, but I can assure you, it really is his hair," Doreen explained with a giggle.

The Indian man never returned to help Betty as he said he would. Betty soon learned that Doreen had been right when she said that the Colorados were indifferent to white people. Every Colorado Indian that Doreen or Barbara asked about being an informant for Betty agreed to come back and help out, but not one of them ever did. Even offering them money for their time did not make a bit of difference.

Betty had other frustrations as well. She had read countless books on missionaries and had met a number of missionaries over the course of her life. Still she was astonished at how much time and energy was taken up as a missionary just doing what was necessary to stay alive. The house had no running water, and water had to be carried in buckets from a river three hundred yards away. Then the water that was to be used for drinking needed to be boiled, as did the milk they drank. All of this took time and energy. As Betty soon learned, milk had to be watched constantly while it was being heated or it would boil over and make a mess.

Lighting the fire and keeping it lit in the stove was also a continual source of stress. Piles of wood had to be gathered and then laid out to dry—not an easy task in the rainy season. And although a thirteen-year-old girl came and did their laundry, scrubbing the clothes clean on a washboard in a tub of water perched over a fire, they still had lots of food preparation to take care of. Every meal they ate had to be made from scratch from what was locally available and cooked over the fogón. And then there was bread to make, which also needed constant watching while it cooked. Betty found it all quite exhausting.

At night the women had limited light to read and write by. The house was lighted by two kerosene lanterns and whatever candles they lit. The trouble was, the light also attracted bugs—lots of them—and the bugs swarmed around the lanterns and candles and whoever happened to be sitting nearby trying to read or write a letter home. All in all, the daily routine of missionary life was a far bigger challenge than Betty had imagined it would be. Sometimes at night she had vivid dreams about visiting a five-and-dime store back home. What a thrill it was to see all those useful items for sale and purchase them in her sleep!

All the while, Betty continued to pray for a Colorado informant to help her in the process of writing down the language. Her prayer was finally answered, but not quite in the way Betty had imagined it might be. She did not find a Colorado Indian to help her. Instead she found a man who spoke the Colorado language fluently and was willing to help as her informant.

Don Macario was a middle-aged Ecuadorian man whom Betty had seen a number of times at the worship service on Sunday mornings. He told Betty that he had been raised on a hacienda (a large plantation) right alongside Colorado children. He had played with them, and in the process he had learned to speak and understand their language fluently. A devout Christian, he was presently unemployed, and he explained that he would be happy to serve as Betty's informant.

Betty was ecstatic when she learned this. God had answered her prayers and sent her possibly the only person in the world who was fluent in both the language of the Colorados and Spanish, which she could speak and understand, making the whole process of communication so much easier for her. She could hardly wait to get to work on the project.

Chapter 11

Unraveling the Language

Betty sat at a long split-bamboo table, her index cards on her left, paper in front of her, and Don Macario on her right. She was making a neat chart of sounds and syllables in the language of the Colorados. One of the first things she had learned from her informant was that the Colorados called the language they spoke *Tsahfihki*—meaning "the language of the people."

Betty and Don Macario soon established a pattern that worked for both of them. They would meet for one hour in the morning, which gave Betty enough material to analyze and categorize for five or six more hours. By then it was time to do the evening chores and set things up for their meeting the next morning.

After a month of meeting regularly each morning with Don Macario, Betty found the work of writing down the language of the Colorados to be progressing slowly but steadily. Her first task was to identify all the various sounds that made up the Tsahfihki language and then reduce them to the least number of symbols, with each symbol representing a particular sound. In this way she was able to produce an alphabet that would one day allow those reading and writing the language to string the various sound symbols together to create words, with which the person could deliver or receive meaning. The words themselves were her next big challenge.

At SIL, Betty had learned that speakers of an unwritten language tend to speak in phrases rather than words and have very little sense of individual words—when words start and when they end. The same was true for Don Macario, who, although he spoke fluent Spanish and was completely familiar with the concept of individual words in Spanish, was hard-pressed to identify individual words in Tsahfihki. He had never seen the language written down and so had never focused on individual words. Like the Colorados, he had learned to speak the language as a series of phrases strung together. It was left to Betty to work through the phrases her informant had spoken and she had written down, searching for what might be the beginning and ending of individual words. Often words have suffixes and prefixes added to them, and Betty looked for repeating patterns in the sounds that might indicate a prefix or a suffix and thus mark the beginning or ending of an individual word. Then she had to work out what those individual nouns and verbs meant in different situations.

Betty kept at the task. She was content with the way things were progressing. From her training at the Summer Institute of Linguistics, she knew that the work of writing down a new language was tedious and often took many detours, but things were moving forward.

Don Macario turned out to be a very patient man, willing to repeat the same sequence over and over until Betty had reduced it to writing. Betty was grateful for his patience with her. She couldn't imagine how difficult it would have been to work with someone impatient or bad-tempered.

Although Betty's main focus was on writing down the language of the Colorados, she was also interested in anything her fellow women missionaries were up to. Sometimes she accompanied Doreen on her jungle missions of mercy or offered to help out in the clinic. So it was not a big surprise when someone banged on Betty's front door late one night.

"Señorita! Señorita!" came a voice.

Betty awoke from a deep sleep, grabbed her robe, and headed for the top of the stairs. "What is it?" she called down.

"It is señor Quiñones. Maruja is in trouble. I think she is dying. Come and help," came the reply.

Knowing that señor Quiñones's wife was pregnant, Betty frowned. This was not the job for a linguist! "Go and wake señorita Barbara," she yelled back. "She can help you better than I." Barbara Johnson had, in fact, been a midwife back in England.

"I have already spoken to her. She is coming, but she told me to come and get you to help her," came the voice in the darkness.

"Wait one minute," Betty said as she turned to hurry to her room and get dressed.

Soon Betty was downstairs, flashlight in hand, walking briskly to the Quiñoneses' house on the other side of the clearing, ready to do whatever she could to assist Barbara. She prayed as she walked. Maruja Quiñones was having her tenth or twelfth baby; she had lost count. Betty knew that Barbara had delivered Maruja's last baby, and things had gone very wrong. The baby had died, and Barbara had made it clear to Maruja and her husband that she would not deliver any more of their babies. Maruja needed to go to a hospital in Quito where they had doctors and equipment to help safely deliver another child. But it was evident that the Quiñoneses had not followed the missionary's advice.

Betty braced herself for what she might find inside. She had helped Barbara out at two previous births, but they had both gone more or less smoothly. She hoped that this one would have a happy ending.

Betty and Barbara were led to a small upstairs room. An oil lamp cast a dull orange glow over the room so that Betty had to strain her eyes to see. Betty was not prepared for what she saw. On a split bamboo bed lay Maruja, crying and wailing. Betty heard a sickly wail behind her and turned to see a baby lying on a pile of rags on the other bed in the room. She walked over to the child, whose chest was barely rising and falling. It did not seem likely to Betty that the baby would survive. But would the mother? Maruja writhed on the bed in agony, making it hard for Barbara to examine her. Her husband tried to comfort her and then broke down in deep sobs and ran from the room. "She's dying!" Betty heard him wail.

"He's right about that," Barbara said calmly and matter-of-factly to Betty in English. "She has a prolapsed uterus. She's in terrible pain and very weak."

"Help me! Please help me!" Maruja screamed. "I can't stand the pain. Please help me!"

Barbara told Betty to warm some plantains in the ashes of the fogón. When Betty had done this, she placed them around Maruja's neck to act as a sort of hot-water bottle, and then they elevated her feet.

"I warned them numerous times that something like this could happen and they should go to a hospital for the delivery. There is little I can do for her here. Her husband will have to take her to the small Catholic hospital in Santo Domingo. Perhaps she will hold onto life until they get there. The jungle women are strong and seem to have a way of holding onto life in the face of the most dire situations."

Betty nodded. She had already noticed that about the women of the jungle.

"I will go and explain the situation to her husband. You stay here and comfort her," Barbara said as she slipped out of the room.

By now Maruja's wails had turned to whimpers. Betty stood close by the bed and tried to comfort her. Then she heard Maruja begin to mumble. Betty leaned in to hear what she was saying.

"Goodbye. Goodbye to all my friends. Goodbye to my family, whom I love. Goodbye to my newborn son, whom God gives and takes away his mother. I commend him to all of you to care for him. I am going now. I bid you all goodbye."

At that moment Maruja's husband entered the room to gather up his wife for the trip to the hospital. He took one look at her and began to wail. "She is already dead! She is already dead!" Tears poured down his cheeks, and he beat the wall with the sides of his fists.

Betty looked down at Maruja. The mouth that only moments before had uttered words was no longer moving. Maruja's jaw was fixed and silent. This was the first dead person Betty had ever seen, and she turned her head away in sadness.

Betty and Barbara slipped out of the Quiñoneses house on the far side of the clearing and made their way to their respective houses. Weary and defeated, Betty paused outside by a bucket of water to wash her hands before going back to bed.

No matter how hard Betty tried, sleep would not come for her. In its place were the hideous scenes of dying mothers, screaming babies, and grown men beating on the walls. The question came to her over and over again: why had God allowed Maruja Quiñones to die? Wouldn't it have been a much better witness if He had miraculously reached down and saved her life, leaving the little baby boy and the dozen or so other children in the house with their mother?

Betty turned over and tried to find a comfortable position. Tears rolled down her cheeks and onto her pillow. In the distance she could hear wailing coming from the direction of the Quiñoneses house as relatives and friends grieved Maruja's death. She could also hear the sound of hammering. A coffin was being constructed for the dead woman.

"So this is missionary life, real missionary life," Betty said to herself under her breath, "with all its frustrations and disappointments, all those feelings of not being able to do enough, to bring enough changes—to really communicate God's love to the people who need it the most.

"Thank God I have my work with Don Macario. At least God answered my prayers and brought me one good person to help me with the task of translation," Betty thought as she finally drifted off into a fitful sleep.

Chapter 12

Jungle Justice

January 25, 1953, was a day Betty Howard would never forget. Betty sat on the end of her bed reading her *Daily Light* devotional book. The verse for the day was from First Peter: "Think it not strange concerning the fiery trial which is to try you, as though some strange thing happened unto you: but rejoice, inasmuch as ye are partakers in Christ's suffering." Betty closed the book and bowed in prayer.

Bang! Bang! Betty cocked her head to listen. She had heard the unmistakable sound of gunshots. The sound was a little closer to the house than usual but nothing too out of the ordinary, since the Colorados and the local men all hunted with guns.

Once again Betty closed her eyes to pray. Then she heard shouts and screams beginning to permeate the air. Next she heard the sound of the hooves of galloping horses and people running. Suddenly the hair on Betty's neck stood up as she heard Doreen scream from downstairs, "They've killed Don Macario!"

Betty sprang from the bed and sprinted down the stairs. "Don't let it be true, don't let it be true," she prayed.

Pulling open the front door, Betty heard a volley of excited voices. "They've murdered Don Macario. Don Macario has been shot!" She stopped, unsure what to do next, when Don Lorenzo, one of the members of the Brethren Assembly, came running up.

"Is it true?" Betty asked.

Don Lorenzo nodded, gasping for breath. It took him several attempts to tell what he knew of the story. Apparently Don Macario and the Quiñones family had quarreled over whether Don Macario or the Quiñoneses had the right to plant banana trees in a cleared patch of jungle close by. As they argued, someone—Don Lorenzo was not sure who—had stepped up and shot Don Macario point-blank. "He dropped down dead. His body still lies over there where he fell." As he spoke, Don Lorenzo pointed to a spot at the edge of the jungle where a crowd had gathered.

"I'm going straight over there," Doreen said.

"No, don't do that," Betty replied. "Wait until we get the authorities. It could be dangerous."

Doreen took no notice and marched off in the direction of the crowd. Betty watched her from the porch of her house. Soon Doreen was back, leading four men, each carrying the corner of a blanket. On the blanket was Don Macario's dead body. Betty let out an involuntary gasp. This was the first time she had ever seen a murder victim.

Before long, Don Macario's body was laid out on Barbara's porch. No one knew what to do with it. One of the women of the village had galloped off to Santo Domingo to get the authorities, and the body could not be buried until some kind of investigation had been undertaken.

In the meantime, the body acted like a magnet to everyone within a five-mile radius of San Miguel. Nursing mothers, small children, old men, and teenage girls all appeared on the porch, eager for a chance to examine the dead body and discuss the circumstances of the death.

The scene repulsed Betty, but she too stayed on Barbara's porch in a personal vigil. She was aware that Don Macario's death had a different implication for her than for anyone else standing around. In front of her lay her link to the Tsahfihki language—and the key to getting a Bible to the Colorado Indians. Don Macario was the only person she knew who was fluent in both Tsahfihki and Spanish. And now he was dead—killed in a senseless act of violence.

Betty thought back to her morning devotion: "Think it not strange concerning the fiery trial which is to try you, as though some strange thing happened unto you: but rejoice, inasmuch as ye are partakers in Christ's suffering." She shook her head. Did Saint Peter really have this in mind when he wrote those words? It was one thing to read about rejoicing when a difficult thing occurred but quite another to rejoice in the midst of such a situation. How could she rejoice when someone had just brutally shot her only informant? How would such an act help to bring the gospel to an isolated people like the Colorados?

Hours passed. Arguments broke out between the mourners and the curious observers. Some said that Don Macario was murdered because he was helping Betty with her translation work; others said that he did not have the right to plant the bananas trees. Betty did not know what to think. She didn't even care about the details of Don Macario's death. All she knew was that a good Christian man who had been willing to help her in her linguistics work was now gone.

It was midafternoon by the time two police officers and another missionary named Bill rode into San Miguel. Betty had not met Bill before, but she had heard about him and how he had served as a missionary in the area for a long time and was familiar with the local customs. She felt relieved, assured that Don Macario's body was now in good hands. However, as was often the case in the jungle, things did not go smoothly.

The taller of the two police officers announced that he could not begin his investigation until he knew what had happened. This made no sense whatsoever to Betty—an investigation was supposed to *find out* what had happened. But there was no reasoning with the officer. And even though he heard from many witnesses as to how the killing had occurred, the officer insisted that someone perform an autopsy and retrieve the bullets so that he could be sure that the man had been shot.

Betty's stomach lurched at the thought, but Bill agreed to perform the autopsy. The scene that followed was one Betty knew she would never forget, even if she wanted to. Bill knelt beside the corpse and after some time was able to locate the bullets. This seemed to satisfy the police officer that Don Macario had been murdered, and now the officer could get on with the investigation.

Betty then turned her attention to the police officers. The officers walked over to the bushes where Don Macario had fallen after being shot, shined their flashlights into them, and then beat the bushes for a minute or so.

"No one is here now," one of the officers declared.

"No one," the other officer agreed. "We have a victim but no suspects," he added, looking up at the sky.

"Too bad we can't stay any longer, but it will be dark soon. We must be going," the first officer commented.

By now Bill had washed himself up as best he could, and he and the two police officers mounted their horses and galloped off in the direction of Santo Domingo.

So that's jungle justice, Betty thought as she watched the men ride away. The police had been more interested in the show than in actually getting to the bottom of what had happened and determining who had committed the murder.

By now the sun had set. Doreen and Barbara got some flashlights and took the body to the schoolroom for the customary wake. Since Don Macario had no family in the area, the members of the Brethren Assembly took charge. Betty took her turn staying part of the night with the body. She joined in the hymn-singing and prayers and the long silences. As the all-night vigil wore on, endless cups of coffee were consumed. Betty could hear the sounds of hammering as a coffin was constructed across the clearing. Early the next morning a funeral service was held, and Don Macario was buried in the small cemetery nearby. Light rain fell as his body was laid to rest, mimicking Betty's gray mood.

After the funeral service, Betty went to her room to rest, but rest would not come. Nightmarish images played before her eyes, and unanswerable questions plagued her. Had the fact that Don Macario was her informant led to his death? Did God care that her one link to the language of the Colorados was gone? Was this part of His plan for the Colorado people, or had Satan just won a huge victory? And how would she overcome her discouragement and find the will to keep going when everything now seemed empty and lost?

No answers to her questions were forthcoming, but Betty found solace in reciting the simple Bible verses that she had learned as a child. She recited the verses like lifelines. "Surely he hath borne our griefs and carried our sorrows...and with his stripes we are healed" (Isaiah 53:4–5) was one of her favorite verses. Yes, she knew she would never understand what had happened, but she would try hard to trust God to help her carry on with her linguistic work.

The following morning Betty pulled out her file box and pen and continued with her work, reviewing the notes and charts of the Tsahfihki language she had made so far. As she worked, she silently prayed that God would show her the way ahead without Don Macario at her side.

Three nights after her informant's murder, Betty once again heard the sound of horses' hooves galloping into the clearing. A friend of Doreen's had come to visit. She also brought with her a telegram that had Betty's name on it. Betty's heart skipped a beat as she opened the telegram. Was someone ill, or dead? What could be so urgent as to warrant a telegram?

A huge smile spread over her face as she read, "Meet me in Quito. Love, Jim."

Suddenly the way seemed clear to Betty. Although she was willing to stay with the Colorado Indians, she had a wonderful feeling that God was unfolding the next stage of His plan for her. She hurried upstairs to pack. She would leave for Quito first thing in the morning.

The next day was one of the longest in Betty's life. She felt like she was moving in slow motion—even the delays had delays. Landslides blocked the way on the truck ride to Quito, and the driver waited endlessly for passengers who waved him down and then disappeared. The chain on the road over the Andes opened late—almost too late to make it to Quito by nightfall. But finally she made it, and two days after receiving the telegram, Betty was in Quito chatting across the table with Jim Elliot. Betty and Jim were at the Tidmarshes' house, where they had been invited to stay.

The dinner conversation was fascinating. Ed McCully and his wife, Marilou, had been invited to dine with the Tidmarshes. Betty knew Ed from Wheaton College. Ed had been in the same year as Jim at college and planned to become a lawyer. In his senior year, Jim had been the president of the Foreign Missions Fellowship, and he had challenged those in the fellowship to target five people and pray that God would call them to be missionaries. Ed McCully was the senior class president, and Jim had targeted him as one of the five people he was praying for. Nonetheless, at the end of his senior year, Ed had not been called to missions but had gone off to earn his law degree at Marquette University. He and Jim had stayed in touch, and somewhere along the way Ed finally felt the call to missionary service. And now here he was in Ecuador. He and Marilou had been in Quito for a month, learning Spanish in preparation for joining Jim and Pete Fleming in the work at Shandia.

Ed and Marilou had many questions about the work at Shandia, and Betty was enthralled as Jim answered them. Jim told how he and Pete had managed to clear the overgrown airstrip at Shandia, making it no longer necessary to make the six-hour trek from the nearest airstrip at Pano to Shandia. Nate Saint, the Missionary Aviation Fellowship (MAF) pilot who serviced the missionaries of the Oriente, could now fly people and supplies in and out of Shandia.

Jim also spoke of a recent experience in which he and Pete had been called out in the middle of the night to try to save the life of a small child sick with pneumonia. They had given the young girl a shot of antibiotics, but despite their best efforts, the child had died. It had been a heartbreaking experience, and Jim explained that he hoped that Ed's presence would vastly improve the quality of the medical care the missionaries could offer at Shandia. Jim explained to Betty that before leaving for Ecuador, Ed had taken a yearlong course at the School of Missionary Medicine in Los Angeles.

When dinner was over, Ed and Marilou returned to the house in which they were staying to check on their nine-month-old son, Steve. The Tidmarshes tactfully retired to their room, leaving Betty and Jim alone together.

A fire crackled in the fireplace as the couple talked. They discussed the similarities and differences of their missionary journeys thus far. After a few minutes their conversation fell silent, and then Jim simply asked, "Betty, will you marry me?"

Betty's heart skipped a beat. This was the moment she had been waiting for! She thought for a moment and then asked, "Jim, do you believe God has given His permission for us to get married and for you to give up the life of a single missionary and take me as your partner?"

Jim nodded, his voice thick with emotion. "Yes, Betty, I do."

That was enough for Betty. "Then the answer is yes."

Their conversation soon turned to practical matters. Jim was adamant that Betty learn to speak the Quichua language before their marriage. He explained that he had seen too many missionary wives who had good intentions but had become weighed down with household duties and babies and never got around to learning the local language. He also said that the wedding could not be anytime soon. He had already committed to building a new house for the McCully family, and he had undertaken several other large projects.

Betty told Jim that she was willing to wait as long as it took, and in the meantime she would begin her Quichua language studies—just as soon as she could figure out a way to do so.

Jim and Betty enjoyed a wonderful week together in Quito: Betty had a ring on her finger and a man at her side. And while in Quito, Betty decided to take advantage of the unexpected trip to civilization and get a medical checkup. On the day that Jim left to return to Shandia to continue with his work there, Betty received some stunning news—a routine chest X-ray had turned up something ominous: an active case of tuberculosis.

Surely not, Betty silently prayed. Was this just another test, another suffering that she had to go through? And how would it affect her plans to marry Jim? There was no way she could go back to the jungle with TB. At the very least she would have to stay and be treated in Quito. Or, if the tuberculosis was too far advanced, she would need to return home to the United States—possibly to die!

Chapter 13

Success and Heartbreak

Betty and Jim began to pray about the situation. They were sure that they were supposed to be married and to work together in the Oriente, but how could that happen now that Betty had tuberculosis? Then, a week after receiving the initial diagnosis, Betty received some great news. No one knew why, but more X-rays showed no TB damage at all to her lungs. Betty wondered—had the first X-ray belonged to someone else, or had God healed her that week? Whatever the case, she was delighted with the outcome.

With a light heart, Betty returned to San Miguel de los Colorados. She was healthy and engaged to Jim. And one day, she hoped not too far in the future, she would be Mrs. James Elliot.

In the meantime, Betty determined to find some way to continue her linguistic work. This was not easy. Now she had to go out to the Colorados in their own homes. The people lived scattered throughout the jungle and spent much of their time either hunting or planting crops away from their houses. More often than not, no one was home when Betty visited. And if someone was home, it was difficult for Betty to communicate her reason for coming. Despite this difficulty, Betty continued to make progress understanding Tsahfihki, jealously guarding every word or phrase that came her way.

It took five more months, but on June 16, 1953, Betty put the finishing touches on the alphabet for the Tsahfihki language. It felt like a huge weight had been lifted from her shoulders. She had forged the first link in the chain that would eventually lead to a translation of the Bible in the language of the Colorados.

Betty now felt sure that it was time for her to move on. The Conns, a missionary family serving with the Christian and Missionary Alliance at Dos Rios in the Oriente, offered her room and board while she learned the Quichua language. Betty eagerly accepted the invitation.

The Conns lived in a delightful spot on the Mishahualli River. A sandy path lined with citrus trees led from the beach on the river to the house set on a hillside overlooking the water. Betty smiled when she saw the clean, white clapboard house with its screened windows. No more bats flying around her room at night!

The Conns were a hospitable family. Everyone knew that Betty wanted to learn Quichua as fast as possible so that she could get married, and Carol Conn spent hours helping her. Betty also enlisted the aid of the kitchen helper and anyone else around who was patient enough to explain the language to her. She made good progress, relieved at how much easier it was to learn a language when others were around to answer questions.

Betty prayed that Doreen, Barbara, and Dorothy back in San Miguel would find small ways to keep adding to the Tsahfihki files she had left with them. She also prayed that someone else with linguistic skills would feel called to go to the village and move the translation work further along. However, Betty was shocked when she read the letter from Doreen Clifford bearing terrible news. In the letter Doreen apologized profusely as she explained how she had taken all of Betty's linguistic notes and materials with her on a bus trip to Quito. She had placed the material in a bag that was slung on top of the bus, but when she arrived in Quito, the bag was gone. Doreen assumed it had been stolen somewhere along the way.

Betty put down the letter and stared out the window, unable to take in what she had just read. What had happened? Where was God in all of this? First her informant was killed, and now her work—the files, the charts, the notebooks—had vanished. The chain, only on its first link, was already broken. Someone else would have to begin again from scratch with the

Tsahfihki language. It was almost too much for Betty to comprehend. Nine months of her life—gone! During the next few days, Betty tried hard to convey in a letter to Jim how she felt. But it was difficult. His work seemed to be progressing nicely at Shandia, while her work had been stripped away from her.

On July 28, 1953, Betty sat at the two-way radio. She often helped Carol Conn out by standing by for the mission updates each morning. All of the missionaries in the area participated. Nate Saint, or more often his wife, Marj, gave an update on the MAF flights for the day. People placed orders for deliveries and asked for prayer and advice on issues that involved them all. Sometimes as she sat by the radio, Betty heard Jim's voice, and it filled her with delight to hear him, but not this day. Jim's voice did come across the airwaves amid a lot of cracking and hissing, but he sounded desperate.

"Shandia to Shell Mera. Shandia to Shell Mera. Over," Jim said over the radio. Betty could hear the franticness in his voice.

After a long pause, Marj's voice came back: "I read you, Shandia. Shell Mera is standing by. Over."

"Marj, bad news. The river is eating away the bluff under the hut. We are only five yards from the edge now. I'll try to keep you posted, but if you don't hear from me at two o'clock, you'll know the house is over the edge. Over."

"Shell Mera reading you, Jim. Will pass the message along. God bless you, and be careful. Over and out," Marj replied.

Betty slumped back in her chair. Tears coursed down her cheeks. What was happening at Shandia? Were Jim and Pete all right? She stayed close to the radio for the next twenty-four hours, hoping Jim would relay another message. The radio was silent. Betty could stand it no longer. Someone had to do something! Betty persuaded a runner for Dos Rios to trek to Shandia to find out what had happened to the missionaries. She sent along with the runner a loaf of freshly made bread for Jim.

Betty had wanted to go along herself, but the Conns would not hear of it. It was the wet season in the Oriente, and there had been a lot more rain lately than normal. The trail would be muddy and difficult to negotiate, especially for someone unfamiliar with it as Betty was.

An agonizing two days passed before the runner returned to Dos Rios with his report. All the missionaries were safe, but their belongings were a different matter. All of the buildings at Shandia had been destroyed, and the flooded Atun Yaku River had swallowed the land on which they had sat. Shandia was no more. The only good news was that many of Jim's and Pete's belongings had been saved, even though they were sodden.

The runner also produced a hurriedly written letter from Jim. The letter was like manna from heaven to Betty. In it Jim described how the bluff that the settlement was built on had given way in the face of the surging river and how all the buildings had been lost along with part of the airstrip. Jim wrote that he doubted a plane could land there now and that the aerial wire needed to send out a radio signal had been lost in the chaos. He also wrote a few private thoughts meant only for Betty. "I wished for some reason that you were here—I do not know why, for we could not have a moment together," Jim wrote.

That was enough for Betty, who sprang into action. She recruited some of the Quichua Christian men from Dos Rios to go back with her to Shandia to find Jim and help him in whatever way they could. They set out that afternoon. The trek was hellish as they slipped and slid through the mud, but Betty was determined to be by Jim's side as quickly as possible.

The next day, Sunday, the group finally arrived at Shandia. The first runner Betty had sent was right: Shandia was no more. Even the land where the mission buildings had stood was gone. The whole place had been obliterated from the face of the earth. Where there had once been land and buildings there was now the angry, flooded Atun Yaku River.

Jim was delighted to see Betty and the group she had brought with her to help. Without a radio antenna or a landing strip, they had been completely cut off from other missionaries and unable to let them know the condition of things at Shandia.

After a happy reunion with Jim, Betty got right to work sorting out wet belongings, discarding ruined items, and draping the rest over bushes to dry.

As she worked, Betty kept a close eye on Jim. He was having trouble walking because his feet were raw, bloodied, and bruised. He'd explained that his feet were in this condition because in the frantic effort to save their belongings he had lost his shoes in the mud and had cut and bruised his feet walking around barefoot in the jungle in the dark. But it wasn't Jim's feet so much that bothered Betty; it was something else. Jim did not seem to be able to concentrate for long. He jumped around in his conversation and sometimes gazed off into the jungle, losing all track of what he was talking about. This was not at all like Jim.

The next day more help arrived in the form of Nate Saint and Dr. Tidmarsh. Nate had landed the MAF plane at Pano, and the two of them had hiked in together to see what they could do to help.

Dr. Tidmarsh frowned when he saw Jim. He took Jim's temperature, asked him a few questions, and then made a pronouncement—malaria! The diagnosis made sense to Betty. No wonder Jim had seemed so distracted.

Dr. Tidmarsh insisted that Jim lie down right away, and he was not to get up until he was told to. Jim did not even argue. He just did what he was ordered to do.

For the next two days Betty looked after Jim as he drifted in and out of consciousness. She was grateful that Nate and Dr. Tidmarsh had come to help her and Pete. Ed also arrived to check out the damage and help wherever he could.

It took a week of Betty's nursing before Jim had the energy to think straight, and then he wanted to talk about only one thing: what did they do next? He questioned the strategy God had in mind for them when He had allowed Shandia to be destroyed.

The men and Betty discussed all sorts of ideas. The most obvious was that perhaps God was trying to spread them out more widely as missionaries. Eventually they reached a consensus that Jim, Pete, and Ed should explore the area around them to see whether God might be leading them somewhere new. Betty agreed to stay at the campsite beside what was once Shandia and take care of their belongings while the three young men mounted an expedition to investigate.

The men set out early one morning in a dugout canoe. Jim was still weak but determined to play his part, though he promised Betty that he would stop and rest if he felt the need to do so. Betty knew that would not happen. Jim's thirst for adventure would win out over resting and napping every time.

Betty wasn't sure how long the men would be gone, but she used the time to continue learning Quichua. Local Christians came every day to sit with her and bring her food, and they were happy to talk with her in their language. As a result, she made rapid progress in learning Quichua.

Twenty-one days after setting out, the men returned. Jim looked fit and well, and the men had a lot to share. The big news was that a Quichua man named Atanasio, who lived in a clearing on the Puyo River, had begged the missionaries to send someone back to start a school for his children and the others in the area. As far as anyone knew, no unchurched Quichua had ever asked white people to come and teach him or her their ways. Jim was jubilant!

As Betty listened to the men talk, it was obvious that they saw Atanasio's school as one of two areas that God wanted them to focus on. The other area of focus was to rebuild Shandia. Betty wondered about who would be assigned to each mission outpost. Jim soon took her aside to explain the situation.

"As we see it, we've already invested a lot of work here in Shandia," Jim began. "The Indians know and trust us, and we shouldn't give that up. It makes sense for Ed and Marilou to move here, especially since they don't know the language yet and the Indians are used to having a missionary around. Of course, Ed will need either Pete or me to stay with him, at least until he knows enough of the Quichua language to get by."

Betty nodded. It made perfect sense to her.

Jim continued. "We also think Atanasio's invitation is a sign from God that we should begin a station down there, too. It would take two people to start the station. The sensible thing would be for Pete to stay here with Ed and Marilou and for me to start the new station. But I'll need a partner."

Betty could feel her heart pounding.

"So…" Jim continued, "how soon will you marry me?"

Chapter 14

Life Together

The marriage of Betty Howard and Jim Elliot took place on October 8, 1953. The ceremony, held at the Registro Civil in Quito, lasted all of ten minutes. Ed and Marilou McCully and Dr. and Mrs. Tidmarsh were the only witnesses. It wasn't the type of wedding every bride would have enjoyed, but it suited Betty, who had no desire to plan a large wedding in the jungle. What mattered most to her was that she and Jim were finally able to embark upon their new life together as a married couple.

Following the wedding, Jim and Betty flew to Panama for their honeymoon and then on to Costa Rica to visit Betty's brother Dave and his wife, Phyllis. Dave and Phyllis were surprised to see Betty and Jim together at their doorstep and even more so when they learned that the two were married. As the word filtered out to relatives and friends about their wedding, Betty and Jim began receiving a steady flow of congratulations and best wishes.

Two weeks after their wedding, the newlyweds were back in Quito working hard to gather the information and supplies needed to set up a new mission station at Atanasio's clearing. The area they were going to was called Puyupungu, and Betty liked the sound of the name. The place would be their first home together.

Both Betty and Jim still had boxes in storage at Quito and had never unpacked some of the things they originally brought with them from the United States. The two of them set to work sorting through their belongings. It was exciting for them to see things they had forgotten they owned. It almost felt like unwrapping wedding presents.

After a few days of unpacking and sorting, they had quite a collection of usable items, including an assortment of garden tools, aluminum cooking pots and pans, a portable stove, and an old tent someone had given Jim before he left Oregon. These items were all duly rewrapped in heavy, waterproof paper, ready to be shipped to their new home in the Oriente.

Once everything had been organized in Quito, Betty and Jim rode the bus down the eastern slope of the Andes to Shell Mera, where Missionary Aviation Fellowship's base of operations in the Oriente was located. Shell Mera was also the home of Nate and Marj Saint and their two children, Kathy and Steve.

Once at Shell Mera, Betty and Jim made preparations for the rest of the journey to their new home.

Puyupungu was not an easy place to get to, even by jungle standards. There was no airstrip into which Nate could fly them, after which they could trek the rest of the way. The only way to Puyupungu, given all the baggage they had to transport with them, was upriver by canoe. Jim set about arranging for canoes to take them to their destination. When everything was organized, Nate drove Jim and Betty to the end of the road, where Betty was relieved to discover the canoes waiting for them. Soon the Elliots' belongings were piled into the canoes, and Betty was waving farewell to Nate. She and Jim were under way on the final leg of the journey to their new home together in the jungle.

The Indians talked and joked as they paddled upriver. Betty could understand some of what they said, but she knew that she would have to continue to study Quichua diligently.

That night Betty and Jim slept in their own "house," a tiny bamboo hut with a thatched roof. Atanasio had made a big ceremony out of presenting the hut to them. Once the Elliots moved in, everyone, including all of Atanasio's wives and children, peered in between the bamboo slats to check on what the strange white people were up to.

Exhausted from the journey upriver, Betty went to sleep that night on a small folding cot, her heart overflowing with gratitude. She awoke about a half hour later with things crawling all over her.

"Jim, light the lamp," Betty whispered.

Soon she wished she had not asked him to do that. Now she could see the hundreds of roaches swarming around in the hut. More dropped down from the thatched roof above them like tiny parachutists. There had been cockroaches at San Miguel, but nothing could have prepared her for this. Betty found it impossible to get back to sleep. Every time she pulled the sheet tightly up over her face, somehow a roach would find a way to crawl under it and across her body.

The next morning Betty talked Jim into pitching the old tent they had brought with them. She explained that she could not cope without sleep, and she would gladly trade a snug-looking hut for a roach-free tent. The tent, a large one, sixteen feet square, proved to be a much better option for living quarters, especially after Jim had outfitted it with a bamboo floor and built a small lean-to kitchen next door.

Jim had just completed building the kitchen when he complained of feeling tired. The next morning he could not get out of bed, and by lunchtime his temperature had soared to 104 degrees Fahrenheit and he was hallucinating. When she saw her husband's condition, Betty was frantic. She gave Jim a shot of antimalarial medicine, but as night fell, Jim's dangerously high temperature continued to rise. She kept a cool, wet cloth on Jim's forehead and prayed throughout the night for him. The next morning she got out the shortwave radio to put in a call to Marj Saint.

This was not easy. The radio took two people to operate—one to turn the crank to generate electricity to run the radio and the other to operate the dials and switches. Betty had learned how to do both at Dos Rios, but now she had to convince someone to continually man the crank. No one seemed to want to help with this repetitious and apparently meaningless task. Eventually one of Atanasio's sons agreed to turn the crank for Betty, who was then able to contact Marj on the radio. Betty described Jim's symptoms to Marj, who was a registered nurse. Betty also told Marj that the antimalarial medicine had not seemed to have any effect and asked whether his condition could be something more than just a relapse of his malaria.

Marj did not know. There was no way of telling without medical tests, and given their location, such tests were out of the question. Marj advised Betty to continue doing what she was doing, keeping Jim cool and comfortable, and wait to see what happened. She also assured Betty that she would ask everyone on the radio link to pray for Jim.

As Betty shut down the radio, she felt her isolation more keenly than ever before. If Jim did need specialized medical help, how would he get it? The easiest way out of Puyupungu was by canoe, and that trip, which took hours, deposited you at a still very remote road head. There was no airstrip for miles, and Marj was the closest medical professional. This was sobering to think about but not something Betty chose to dwell on as she nursed her sick husband.

For the next three weeks, Betty sat beside Jim, keeping damp cloths on his forehead, spooning liquids into his mouth, and praying as he writhed and groaned on his bed. The rains came, and Betty had to move everything into the middle of the tent, since anything that touched the tent sides quickly became soaked through.

Finally Jim began to show signs of improvement. He asked the date and was shocked to learn just how long he had been drifting in and out of consciousness.

When Jim felt well enough again, he set about building a schoolhouse while Betty compiled the materials necessary to teach Atanasio's twelve children. Atanasio also wanted to come along to school, and Betty encouraged him to do so.

Once the schoolhouse was completed, Betty started giving simple Quichua lessons. First everyone had to learn the alphabet and grasp the concept that words went from left to right across the page. Betty taught the sounds that went with each letter and how to string the sounds together to make syllables and then whole words. The work was slow but rewarding, especially since Jim had started translating the Gospel of Luke into Quichua. Betty imagined the day when her students would be able to read the book for themselves.

As Christmas 1953 approached, the Elliots decided they needed some encouragement and fellowship, and they accepted the McCullys' invitation to come to Shandia for Christmas. On the morning of December

18, Betty and Jim set out on the journey to Shandia. Ahead of them lay a long trek on an overgrown jungle trail to Puyo. They hired a Quichua guide to lead them on the trail, and before long Betty realized just how overgrown it was. The guide and Jim had to hack away with machetes to clear patches of the trail—exhausting work in the jungle heat. The trail was not situated on the lowlands but followed the Indian tradition of building their trails on the highest ground possible so that it would not become flooded in the rainy season. Of course, this meant that they had to scramble up every hill and incline along the way. Nonetheless, the beauty of the jungle entranced Betty. Huge water plants and vines hung from trees, and everything was green and leafy. The jungle was abuzz with the sound of wildlife around them: chattering monkeys, croaking tree frogs, and squawking parrots.

After nine hours of trekking through the jungle, they emerged into a field of sugarcane. Beyond the sugarcane was Puyo, and waiting to meet them in Puyo was Marj Saint. Better still, Marj had several bottles of cold Coca-Cola and some slices of chocolate cake with her. Coca-Cola had never tasted so good to Betty as it did at that moment. Marj drove Betty and Jim to Shell Mera, and the next morning Nate flew them to Shandia, landing on the newly repaired airstrip.

It felt good to be back at Shandia, and Betty marveled at how different the place looked from how it had looked after the flood. Pete and Ed had been busy clearing jungle and constructing new living quarters. They all had a great time celebrating Christmas together and catching up with each other. Pete was making final preparations to return to the United States for several months. He planned to marry his childhood sweetheart, Olive Ainslie, and return to the Oriente with her. Betty and Jim were delighted to catch up with him before he left.

Betty and Jim ended up staying in Shandia until January 5, 1954. They stayed on to help out at Shandia's first ever Bible conference. The event sounded grander than it was, but during the conference many Quichua Christians were challenged to take the gospel to their own people instead of relying on foreign missionaries to do the job. Jim had the joy of baptizing two women, Eugenia Cerda and Carmela Shiwangu. The conference was a happy occasion for all the missionaries in the area, and Betty looked forward to seeing many more Quichuas become Christians and be baptized.

The success of the Bible conference caused the missionaries to rethink their plans for the future. There was more Christian growth at Shandia than at any of the other stations, and since the aim of the missionaries was to train Quichuas to become missionaries to their own people, it made a lot of sense to make Shandia their central mission base.

With this goal in mind, Jim and Betty decided that once the first school year was finished at Puyupungu, they should relocate back to Shandia and then work part-time at Puyupungu. In this way the students at Puyupungu could still have classes, and Jim and Betty would be freed up to help disciple and encourage the Quichua Christians at Shandia.

Refreshed and encouraged by this new vision, Betty and Jim trekked back to Puyupungu. Jim set about building a permanent house for them beside the river. He also began laying out a site for an airstrip that would make it easy for him and Betty to get in and out of the place. By Easter, both tasks were completed ahead of schedule. Many local men had come from Pano to help Jim do the work.

Just as Jim was finishing the screened windows on the house, he and Betty received a letter from Oregon. Every letter in their isolated jungle home was a welcome one, but this one was especially so. It was from Jim's father, who wrote that he was coming down to visit them in Ecuador. He was planning to stay a month, during which time he wanted to be involved in a building project. With the house and the airstrip finished, Puyupungu had no immediate need for more building projects, and Betty's thoughts immediately turned to Shandia.

With its new designation as the center of missionary work for the area, additional simple housing was needed at Shandia. Betty asked Jim whether he thought his father would be interested in helping with a building project there. After several radio conversations with the other missionaries, everyone agreed that Betty and Jim would move back to Shandia when the school semester was over, and Jim's father would join them and build a house for them.

Betty had also just learned that she was expecting a baby early in the new year. She was thrilled to think that she would have the added blessing of being around other young missionary mothers. It was difficult enough for an adult, much less a newborn baby, to stay healthy in the jungle. Marj and Marilou would provide Betty with strong shoulders to lean on.

In May, Jim and Betty left Puyupungu behind and made their way to Shell Mera, where Jim's father was waiting for them. It was a happy reunion. To top things off, Jim's dad had brought a lot of construction equipment with him, including gasoline-powered saws and drills, which would make the construction job much easier.

Life at Shandia soon fell into a pleasant rhythm. Betty and Jim stayed in a tiny bamboo hut that Pete had built, and Jim's father stayed in a hut in the clearing. They all ate with the McCullys, and during the day Jim and his dad and a group of Indians worked hard at the construction of a new house for the Elliots. The house was situated in the jungle, a twelve-minute walk from the clearing at Shandia. First the site had to be cleared of jungle, and then sand and rocks were brought from the river to make concrete for the foundation of the new house. It was hard, hot work, and in the afternoons Betty would walk to the construction site with a large pitcher of lemonade for the men to drink. Just before the sun went down Jim would return to their tiny hut and bathe in the river, and then he and his dad and Betty would eat with the McCullys. In the evenings Betty and Jim would write letters home, prepare Bible studies for the local Christians, or sometimes just sit and talk with the McCullys.

The weeks flew by. Before long Betty and Jim were celebrating their first wedding anniversary, and in December Marilou gave birth to a second son. Once the construction of a modest home for Betty and Jim was complete, Jim's father returned to the United States. Betty loved the house. It even had a room for Betty to prepare as a nursery.

In February 1955, Betty and Jim went to stay at Shell Mera. Betty had decided not to go to Quito to give birth to the baby but rather to go to Shell Mera and trust Marj to be her midwife. This proved to be a good decision, and on February 27 Valerie Elliot was safely born. She had white-blonde hair and very pink skin, something that Betty knew would make the child an instant hit with the Quichua Indians in Shandia. And so it was. When the Elliot family arrived back at Shandia, everyone wanted to tickle Valerie's toes and stroke her fine hair. Few of them had ever seen a white baby before.

Soon after the Elliots' arrival back at Shandia, Betty's parents came to visit to see their new granddaughter. On their way to Ecuador, the Howards stopped in Costa Rica to visit Betty's brother Dave and his wife, Phyllis.

Betty was glad to see her parents when they arrived. Her parents doted over Valerie, and Betty was able to show them all the progress that was being made in sharing the gospel with and discipling the local Quichua Indians. In the evenings they all loved to sit and talk in the Elliots' new home. During these times, Betty's parents filled her in on all the family news. One piece of particularly exciting news was that Betty's younger sister Ginny, her husband Bud DeVrie, and their baby Kenny were leaving the United States in April for Palawan in the Philippines, where they would serve as missionaries with the Association of Baptists for World Evangelism.

During the visit Betty noticed that her father was not quite his old self. He had always been an inquisitive man, interested in people and the things going on around him, but now he just sat and stared. Betty spoke to her mother about this, but neither of them knew why he was acting the way he was.

After her parents had returned to the United States, Katherine Howard wrote to say that Betty's father had been diagnosed with a brain tumor. He had emergency surgery to remove the tumor, and Betty's mother reported that he was recovering well and was back to his old self. Betty breathed a sigh of relief and prayed a prayer of gratitude.

Meanwhile, the mission work at Shandia was progressing nicely. Ed and Marilou were preparing to occupy a second outstation at a place called Arajuno, an old Shell Oil exploration base. Located just across the river from a large Quichua Indian village, the base had been abandoned in 1949. The McCullys planned to establish a school and church among the Quichua there. But before they could move, a house had to be built for the family at the site. Fortunately, the Shell Oil Company had left behind a well-formed, packed-sand airstrip, and Nate had offered to fly Ed in and out of the site and help him build a house there for the family. With the new house nearly complete and the McCully family getting ready to move into it, Betty found herself confronting some difficult questions.

While Arajuno was located opposite a large Quichua village, it was also located just outside Auca territory. Long ago Jim had confided to Betty that his ultimate dream was to reach the Auca Indians with the gospel. But the Aucas were not like the Quichuas, who wore Western-style clothing and were friendly toward outsiders. The Aucas wore only a woven string around their waist and had balsa wood plugs in the lobes of their ears. They also had a fearsome reputation as vicious killers. Their mentality seemed to be kill or be killed—not only other Aucas but also outsiders, including Shell Oil Company workers. The brutal attacks were one of the reasons the company had decided to abandon its base at Arajuno.

On numerous evenings at Shandia, Jim, Ed, and Pete had sat together talking about the Aucas and strategizing about the best way to make friendly contact and take the gospel to them. Now that the work at Shandia was progressing well, Betty wondered what might lie ahead for her and Jim. What would happen if they did make friendly contact with the Aucas? Was she prepared to take Valerie and go and live with them? If reaching them was really Jim's vision, could she embrace that vision as well?

Betty was not sure of the answers to those questions, and she was grateful that, for the time being, she did not have to make any decisions. There was still plenty of work at Shandia to keep her and Jim busy.

Chapter 15

Operation Auca

There's been an Auca attack at Arajuno!" Jim told Betty as she hung out the laundry to dry. "Marj just sent word on the radio."

Betty put down the clothespins and turned to face her husband. "What else did she say?"

"That they killed a Quichua mother and her two children and took off with a stolen canoe."

The news of the attack had a chilling effect on the young missionary couples at Shandia. The men had been talking for weeks about strategies for making contact with the Aucas and reaching out to them with the gospel. The McCully family were in the final stages of preparing to move to Arajuno—the very place where the Aucas had killed a defenseless woman and her two children. No one said it, but it was easy to imagine Marilou and her two children in that same situation.

It was time for them all to seriously pray about the situation. Betty knew that everyone was aware that reaching out and making contact with the Aucas was a risky thing to do—foolhardy even—unless God specifically spoke to them and guided them forward.

After praying about the matter, the McCullys did finally move to Arajuno, but not before Nate had set up an electric fence around their new house that the family could use for protection at night. The Aucas had never encountered electricity, and an unexpected zap from the fence would surely deter them from coming any closer.

At the same time, Pete and his new bride, Olive, who had recently returned to the Oriente from the United States, decided to go and man the outpost at Puyupungu. The vision of Shandia being the hub in a wheel of mission outposts was becoming a reality.

Betty and Jim were busier than ever at Shandia running a school, church, and part-time medical clinic. In July 1955, Jim's brother Bert and his wife, Colleen, came to visit from Peru. Jim and Betty took the opportunity to show Bert and Colleen all the things that had happened since they had moved to Shandia. They all stood and watched as fourteen people were baptized in the river, and Nate was able to fly them around to the mission outposts to encourage the missionaries there. On the trip they learned the McCullys had not encountered any hostile Aucas and that they had made many friends among the Quichua Indians in the area.

Still, at the back of everyone's mind was the idea that one day—somehow—God was going to bring the gospel to "the neighbors," as Ed liked to call the Aucas.

Things began to fall into place on September 15, 1955, when Nate and Ed were flying over the jungle. From the air Ed spotted a cultivated clearing ringed with thatched-roof huts. The men had found a group of elusive Aucas!

Two weeks later Jim and Betty learned that a second Auca village, only fifteen minutes from Arajuno, had been spotted from the air. It was astonishing to the Elliots that Auca settlements had been spotted twice in two weeks. Nate had spent seven years flying over the same jungle and had never seen any signs of them before. Was God trying to tell them something? Was He perhaps leading them to prepare for contact with this Stone Age tribe? Neither Betty nor Jim knew for sure, but they both were excited about the possibilities that lay ahead.

After the discovery of the two Auca villages, things began to move quickly. Ed and Nate continued to fly over the Auca settlements, even dropping gifts to the people below. To do this they used a unique spiral-line drop system that Nate had developed. This involved lowering a bucket on a line from a circling airplane. As the bucket neared the ground, its swinging motion would get smaller and smaller until the bucket was almost still while the plane circled above. This meant that gifts could be sent down to the Aucas, who in turn could place things in the bucket if they wanted to. It was a red-letter day when Nate sent word that the neighbors had sent up a parrot in the bucket!

The work at Shandia continued. Betty and Jim were in the process of discipling about twenty Quichua Christians, many of whom were now able to read for the first time. The Quichuas attended group Bible studies and one-on-one sessions with the Elliots to improve their skills. Jim and Betty hoped that soon these local Christians would be able to take over the work of preaching and teaching in the church. They realized that this was the fastest and best way to grow the local church. Also, a new building was taking shape at Shandia. A cement floor had just been poured for a new and permanent schoolhouse. In addition, keeping the airstrip in good repair was no easy task in the dense jungle.

In October, Jim made a four-hour trek to Hacienda Ila, where Dayuma, an Auca woman, lived. Betty would have loved to accompany him, but they did not want to raise suspicions about their possible efforts to make contact with the Aucas.

Ordinarily, Rachel Saint, Nate's older sister, lived on the plantation at Hacienda Ila, where she was working with Dayuma to decode the Auca language. Nate had indicated that Rachel was away for a time, attending a conference in Quito. Rachel was a missionary with Wycliffe Bible Translators. She had worked among the Shapra Indians in Peru for many years. When Ecuador's president invited Wycliffe missionaries to come and work in his country, Rachel had made the move to Ecuador. She, too, had a deep desire to see the gospel spread among the Aucas. When she learned about an Auca woman named Dayuma living and working at Hacienda Ila, she came to live at the hacienda and learn all she could about the Auca language from Dayuma.

After much soul-searching, those involved in Operation Auca (as their plan to make contact with the Aucas was now called) agreed that it would be best to keep their plan secret. Anyone not immediately involved in it did not need to know what was going on, and that included Rachel Saint.

So with Rachel away, Jim made his trip to Hacienda Ila. He was very excited upon his return from his visit with Dayuma. He told Betty that Dayuma had fled the Auca tribe as a young child, and although she'd forgotten some Auca words, she was very helpful. Jim pulled out his black notebook and began reading to Betty a list of phrases Dayuma had taught him.

"*Biti miti punimupa* means 'I like you. I want to be your friend.' *Biti winki pungi amupa* means 'I want to come near you' or maybe 'Let's get together.' I am not sure yet. And if I say *Awum irimi,* that means 'What is your name?'"

Betty was fascinated by the first few words of this new language. She decided that if Jim visited Dayuma again, she would go with him. In her heart she knew that it was more a question of *when* than *if*. Jim had come back too excited to even eat dinner. All he could talk about was the way these simple phrases would help him and the other men reach the Aucas.

As December rolled around, Jim took some flights with Nate, and he was able to see the Aucas for himself. He even got to speak to the Aucas over a loudspeaker, repeating some of the phrases he'd learned from Dayuma. Betty watched as his eyes glistened when he told her about the experience.

One day Betty decided to ask her husband the question that had been haunting her for weeks now. "Jim, I understand that someone has to bring the gospel to the Aucas, but I need to ask you this: are you sure that *you* are supposed to go?"

"I am called," Jim replied simply.

Betty nodded. That was all she needed to know. The mission was a dangerous one. There was no doubt that one or all of the men could lose their lives in the process. But if Jim knew beyond a doubt that he was called to go, Betty was sure she could live with whatever the outcome might be.

A few days later, Betty trekked to Hacienda Ila with Jim. She was delighted to meet Dayuma, whom she discovered also spoke fluent Quichua. Betty studied Dayuma, a short, dark woman with high cheekbones. The only thing that really marked Dayuma as different from the Quichua Indians working at Hacienda Ila was her earlobes. As young children, Aucas had their ears pierced, and small balsa wood plugs were inserted into the holes. Over time these balsa wood plugs were changed for larger plugs until by the time the children were teenagers, the holes in their earlobes were the size of a silver dollar. Dayuma's earlobes were the same, except that she no longer wore plugs in her ears. As a result, her earlobes were loose and dangly.

Dayuma told Betty about fleeing from her tribe when another Auca killed her father. She said that she feared for her life in the bloody round of revenge killing that was sure to follow her father's death. For the past eight years she had worked on the plantation at Hacienda Ila.

By the time Betty and Jim left the hacienda to trek back to Shandia, Jim had many more Auca phrases jotted down in his black notebook.

The Elliots spent Christmas 1955 with the McCullys and the Flemings at Arajuno. Most of the conversation during their stay centered around Operation Auca. Nate had reported to the men that he'd found a sandy beach on the Curaray River near one of the Auca settlements. He was confident that he could land his Piper Cruiser on the beach. The plan to venture into Auca territory and make first contact with the people was unfolding better than anyone could have imagined.

The plan called for Nate to fly the men to the beach, which they now referred to as Palm Beach, on the Curaray River. The men would build a house in a tree at the end of the beach in which they would sleep at night. During the day they would wait on the beach for the Aucas to come to them so that they could make contact with them. They hoped that the list of Auca phrases Jim had collected and practiced would help them communicate that they had come in peace and meant the Aucas no harm. In the evening Nate would fly back to Arajuno and sleep the night there, leaving the others to spend the night in the tree house on Palm Beach. Nate was concerned about leaving the airplane on the beach overnight. If it rained in the night, the river could flood and wash the aircraft away. Or under the cover of dark the Aucas could damage or destroy the plane.

The day after New Year's Day, the men would gather at Arajuno, the staging ground for Operation Auca, and Nate would ferry them and their supplies to Palm Beach.

By now Nate had recruited another participant for Operation Auca, Roger Youderian. Roger and his wife, Barbara, were missionaries among the Jivaro Indians to the south. Roger had been a paratrooper in the Second World War, and Nate felt he would be a great addition to the team. This brought the number of men participating in Operation Auca to five. This created a problem, however. Jim had already prefabricated the tree house they would build in the tree at the end of the beach. But he had anticipated only three people sleeping in it at night and had designed it accordingly. The tree house would have no room for an extra person to sleep. It was decided that since Pete was the lightest of the men of Operation Auca, he would fly out with Nate each night and sleep over at Arajuno.

Betty joined in the conversation among the men whenever she could and spent the rest of the time helping with the meals and watching the children—ten-month-old Valerie, along with Stevie and Mike McCully.

After enjoying a delicious Christmas dinner prepared with supplies Nate had flown in especially for the occasion, the Elliots returned to Shandia to conduct the end-of-year Bible conference. The conference was a great success, and Betty marveled at the spiritual growth she saw in the lives of the young Quichua Christians who attended.

The Bible conference ended on New Year's Day 1956. When everyone attending had departed, Betty turned her attention fully to Jim's needs. January 2 was the day the five men were scheduled to meet at Arajuno. Operation Auca would begin the following day.

Coincidentally, Rachel Saint had been asking about how the missionary work at Shandia was progressing, and Betty had invited her to come and see for herself. Rachel had accepted the invitation and decided to visit Shandia at the same time Operation Auca was about to begin. This posed a problem, since Rachel had been told nothing about the operation. Because Jim wanted things to stay that way, he led Rachel to believe that he was off to run a weeklong series of meetings at Arajuno and that it would be a great idea for her to stay with Betty at Shandia while he was away.

Betty helped Jim pack a few clothes, along with anything she could think of that might interest and amuse the Aucas Jim and the men hoped to meet.

Among the things she helped him pack were a har-
monica, a View-Master with several different picture
reels, and a yo-yo. She watched while Jim slid the
last item into the pocket of his bag—a small pistol.
Betty knew that the men had agonized over whether
or not to take the weapon with them. After all, they
were coming in peace to make contact with the
Aucas, yet they also realized that the jungle was a
dangerous place. Pumas, alligators, and snakes were
sure to be lurking around Palm Beach, and the men
needed some way to protect themselves. In the end
they decided that they would take the gun for protection, but under no circumstances would they fire it at
the Aucas if they were attacked. If it came to losing
their own lives or taking the life of an Auca, the men
all agreed that for the sake of the gospel they would
choose to lay down their lives.

Finally everything was ready. Nate radioed that
he and Rachel were ten minutes away in the plane.
Betty's heart beat hard at the news. She picked up
Valerie and walked outside, turning just as Jim closed
the door behind him. A chill ran down Betty's spine.
"Do you realize that you may never open that door
again?" was what Betty wanted to say to her husband, but she kept silent. She knew that Jim did not
need an emotionally distraught wife right now. His
mind was totally settled on this course of action, and
she determined to support him in it.

Jim and Betty walked to the airstrip just as the
yellow MAF Piper Cruiser circled for a landing. Betty
shifted Valerie from one hip to the other and waited.

Soon the plane was on the ground and had taxied to a halt. Rachel and Nate climbed from the plane, and the four of them had a brief conversation. Then Jim kissed Betty, threw his bag into the back of the plane, and clambered into the right front seat. Nate cranked the engine back to life, and with a wave the men sped off down the airstrip. Betty watched the plane lift off and then bank in the direction of Arajuno.

As she escorted Rachel back to the house, Betty prayed for Operation Auca. "Have Your way, Lord, have Your way."

The next few days were difficult for Betty, who had to continue as normal, since Rachel was with her and there was little radio contact because everything was kept secret. Marj did manage to keep Betty partially updated with a few coded messages. In one message she stated that Nate had spotted a "commission of ten" coming from "terminal city." Betty knew that this meant that ten Aucas had been spotted coming toward the men from the nearby Auca settlement.

On Wednesday, January 4, 1956, Nate flew into Shandia and delivered a note from Jim to Betty that filled her in on what had happened so far. Betty quickly unfolded the note and read. Jim explained that things were going well at Palm Beach. Nate had ferried them and their things in flawlessly, and they had set to work building the tree house. The house was located thirty-five feet above the beach, and getting it up there had been quite a struggle. But now that it was up, it was comfortable and safe and well worth the effort. In the night they had heard the sound of a puma and discovered its tracks on the beach in the morning. It was also much hotter at Palm Beach than at Shandia, and Jim and the others were perspiring a lot. Jim ended his note by saying that they had seen no sign of the neighbors, but they were hopeful that they would show up. In fact, the men were about to descend to the beach with the gifts and novelty items Jim had brought along and wait to see whether any Aucas showed up. When Betty had read the note, Nate added that they were hoping for contact with the Aucas the next day.

On January 6, Rachel and Betty waited for the radio to beep—Rachel because she expected Marj to call and tell her that Nate was in the area and would soon be landing to pick her up and fly her back to Shell Mera, and Betty because she had not heard an update on the men since the day before.

Betty looked at the clock. She had expected a call around four o'clock in the afternoon, and now it was four thirty. Betty tried to shake off the feeling of gloom that engulfed her; surely she would hear from Marj soon. Valerie cried, and Betty got her up from her nap and fed her.

It was 4:45 PM when Betty decided that it was time to contact Marj herself. She went to the radio and spoke into the microphone. "Shell Mera, this is Shandia. Come in please."

At first Betty heard nothing but static and crackle, and then she heard Marj's voice. "I read you, Shandia."

"Any news?" Betty asked, being careful not to say anything specific about Operation Auca.

After a second's hesitation, Marj replied, "No news of the boys. Sorry I can't tell you anything. Nate has not come back. Johnny Keenan, our reserve pilot, is going to fly over the Curaray at first light to see if he can spot anything. Over."

Betty and Marj chatted for a couple more minutes, and then Betty put down the radio microphone. What had happened to the men? Perhaps the little yellow Piper Cruiser had become bogged down in the sand and they were all going to have to walk out from Palm Beach. Or perhaps something more sinister had happened. Betty explained to Rachel that the plane had been delayed, which was technically true.

Betty spent a fitful night tossing and turning in bed and praying for good news in the morning.

Chapter 16

Tragic News

Betty strained to hear what Marj was saying through the static. "Johnny has found the plane on the beach. All of the fabric is stripped off it. There is no sign of the men. Over."

Betty's hand flew to her face at the news. She turned and saw Rachel standing in the doorway. "I copy you, but I have to go, Marj. Rachel is here. Can Johnny come and get us? I think we should all be together right now. Over." Betty said over the radio, her voice quivering.

"I was thinking the same thing. I'll radio you back when he's in the air. Over and out."

Betty pushed back her chair and slowly stood. She took a deep breath. "I'm sorry, Rachel. I didn't want you to have to find out this way," she said, "but

173

the men are in trouble. We've lost radio contact with them, and it doesn't look good."

Rachel stared at Betty, her eyes wide with disbelief. "Why didn't you say anything sooner?" she asked.

Betty poured a cup of coffee and then sat down and began unraveling the whole story to Rachel. As she spoke, she could see the hurt in Rachel's expression at not having been informed what her brother was up to and not having been told the reason that she and Jim had visited her informant Dayuma.

There was little Betty could do now except explain as best she could that Jim and the other men involved in Operation Auca had agreed to total secrecy, which included not telling their churches back home, their parents, or even their senior missionary, Dr. Wilfred Tidmarsh.

The radio burst to life again just as Betty finished explaining things to Rachel. Marj was calling to inform them that Johnny was on his way to Shandia to collect them. Betty threw a few things into a bag for herself and Valerie, and then the three of them headed down the track to the airstrip. So much had happened since the last time Betty had walked down this same track with Jim.

Johnny brought the plane in for a landing, and Rachel and Betty, with Valerie on her hip, climbed in. Moments later they were airborne. Betty looked down at the dense jungle as it passed below them. Was Jim somewhere out there trying to get back to her? The three adults in the airplane sat in silence for most of the twenty-minute flight. What was there to say? Johnny had not spotted any of the men, and there had been no word from them. Betty comforted herself with the knowledge that if the men had fled when the plane was attacked, it would take them over a day on foot to reach civilization. It was too soon to draw any conclusions.

Johnny dropped Betty, Valerie, and Rachel at Shell Mera and took off to pick up the other wives, Marilou McCully, Olive Fleming, and Barbara Youderian.

Marj welcomed Rachel and Betty to the house and apologized to Rachel for her having to find out about Operation Auca in such a difficult manner. Rachel did not want to talk about it, and a tense silence pervaded the room. Valerie crawled around after Kathy Saint, who was supposed to be celebrating her seventh birthday that day.

Things at the MAF house in Shell Mera remained solemn. A single question hung in the air: what should they do next? No one seemed to know what the best thing to do would be. Should they contact the Ecuadorian army? The United States embassy? The local police?

As the women sat pondering their next move, they heard a knock at the door. Betty and Marj turned toward the door at the same moment. Perhaps it was the men! Marj rushed to open the door, and there stood Larry Montgomery, a pilot for Wycliffe Bible Translators. Marj invited him in.

Larry quickly explained why, unexpectedly, he was at Shell Mera. "I was passing through Quito, and I had the strangest feeling that I should get on a bus and come visit you folks. It took thirteen hours to get here, and I apologize for not letting you know I was coming."

Betty and Marj looked at each other in amazement.

"Come in and sit down, Larry," Marj said. "We have something to tell you."

Soon the story of Operation Auca tumbled out. Larry sat and listened, occasionally interjecting a question for clarification of some point. He wanted to know how long it had been since Johnny had spotted the plane on Palm Beach and whether the aircraft looked as if it had been wrecked before its fabric skin was stripped off.

When Betty and Marj had told him what they could, Larry stood and said, "If you will allow me, I think the best thing would be to contact my friend General Harrison by shortwave radio. General Harrison is the U.S. military officer in charge of the Caribbean region. He's a devout Christian, and I know he will help us."

Marj nodded, and Larry walked to the radio room, just off the kitchen. Betty listened as Larry picked up the microphone and began calling out on the radio. Within half an hour he was talking directly to General Harrison. Tears of relief welled in Betty's eyes. An hour ago she and Marj were agonizing over what to do next, and now Larry Montgomery was on the radio talking to a high-ranking U.S. military officer.

From that moment on everything began to move swiftly at Shell Mera. General Harrison told Larry that he would instruct Air Force Major Nurnberg, based in

Panama, to initiate an immediate search-and-rescue mission. The U.S. Air Force was on its way.

Eventually the other three wives, along with their children, arrived at Shell Mera. And by evening, as word got out about the missing men, people began to converge on Shell Mera.

On Tuesday night, two Air Force C-47 cargo planes touched down at Shell Mera from Panama. One of the planes carried Major Nurnberg and a rescue team; the other, an H-13 helicopter. The following morning the helicopter was unloaded, and a crew began assembling it for flight.

Grady Parrott, the president of Missionary Aviation Fellowship, flew in directly from California, followed by two officials from Christian Missions in Many Lands, the organization the Elliots, the McCullys, and the Flemings served with in Ecuador. Several missionary friends from Quito also hurriedly made their way to Shell Mera to help.

The MAF house at Shell Mera continued to fill up with even more people. Sam Saint, Rachel and Nate's brother and an experienced pilot with American Airlines, arrived to lend his support. He was followed by Jerry Hannifin, foreign correspondent for *Time* magazine, and then came Cornell Capa, the famous *Life* magazine photographer. As well, HCJB, the Christian radio station in Quito, was relaying updates around the world.

All of this passed by Betty and the other wives in a blur. The women did what they had to do—bathe babies, wash loads of diapers, and feed everyone—but their hearts were with their husbands. If only they knew where the men were and whether they were safe. Eventually Marilou insisted on being flown back to Arajuno. She was convinced that any survivors among the men would head for her house, since it was the closest to Auca territory.

A search party led by Frank Drown, Roger Youderian's co-missionary, was formed, and several other missionaries and thirteen Ecuadorian soldiers bravely headed out on foot from Arajuno into the jungle. Meanwhile, search planes made low passes over the area looking for any sign that the men were alive.

On Wednesday morning, January 11, 1956, two days after the news that Nate's plane had been spotted on Palm Beach stripped of its fabric skin, Betty was upstairs with Barbara and Olive. Suddenly Marj's urgent cry filled the room. "Betty! Barbara! Olive!"

Betty raced down the stairs, with Barbara and Olive right behind her. Marj was standing with her head in her hands. Her eyes were closed. Betty waited, heart pounding, and then Marj finally spoke. "They found one body."

Marj went on to explain what she knew from Johnny's radio call. Johnny was flying over Palm Beach again and spotted one body floating facedown in the river about a quarter of a mile downstream. The body was clad in khaki pants and a white T-shirt. Betty's mind raced. Jim had taken khaki pants and a white T-shirt with him, but then she quickly learned that so had all the other men except Roger.

Later in the afternoon, the radio crackled again—more bad news. Johnny had spotted a second body floating in the river about two hundred yards from the beach.

On Thursday, the helicopter and the Air Force planes were in the air and headed for the site where the two bodies had been spotted. That night, Major Nurnberg and another Air Force officer, Captain DeWitt, flew to Shell Mera. The major had a solemn look on his face. "Is there somewhere privately we could meet with the wives?" he asked Marj.

Marj nodded and turned to lead them upstairs to her bedroom.

Some of the wives sat on the bed and others preferred to stand as Major Nurnberg cleared his throat. Betty knew he was about to deliver bad news—very bad news.

And so it was. Jim was dead. All of the men were dead—killed by Auca spears. Four of the bodies had been spotted from the air by the helicopter, and a fifth body, that of Ed McCully, had earlier been discovered by a canoe party of Quichua Indians. The major explained that the Quichuas were Christians from Arajuno, and when they learned their missionary was missing, they loaded into two canoes and headed downstream in search of him, even if it meant crossing into Auca territory. They had made it all the way to Palm Beach, where they found Ed's body at the water's edge. After discovering the fate of their missionary, they took Ed's watch from his wrist and made their retreat from Auca territory. On the way upriver, they met the ground search party headed for Palm Beach. They told Frank Drown about finding Ed's body and handed Ed's wristwatch to him.

It was a solemn moment as Major Nurnberg read the descriptions of the bodies from his small notebook and each wife identified her husband from the description.

When the major had finished, there was nothing more to say. After twenty-seven months of marriage, Betty was now a widow and the single mother of a ten-month-old daughter. Olive Fleming was a widow. Marj Saint was a widow with three children; Marilou McCully, a widow with two children and another on the way; and Barbara Youderian, a widow with two children. In an instant their worlds had changed forever.

The next few days were a blur of activity. On Friday the ground search party made it to Palm Beach and recovered the bodies from the water. The party was able to find only four of them: the river had washed away Ed's body. A mass grave was dug at the foot of the tree in which the tree house was located, and the four men were buried there. Before their bodies were lowered into the common grave, Frank Drown took the men's wedding rings and whatever else the men had in their pockets to return to the widows. A tropical rainstorm burst over Palm Beach as the bodies were buried.

When he arrived back at Shell Mera, Frank handed Jim's wristwatch to Betty, along with some torn-out pages from Jim's prayer notebook. He had also located Nate's waterlogged camera, still with film inside it, from where it had fallen into the river.

On Saturday, six days after the men had gone missing, Betty and the other wives were flown over Palm Beach in a U.S. military aircraft to see the site of the killing for themselves. Betty peered down at the peaceful sight of Palm Beach below. She could see on the sand the skeleton of the little yellow MAF Piper Cruiser that she and Jim had flown in so many times. She could see the cooking shelter that Jim had sketched out on the kitchen table weeks before back in Shandia and the prefabricated tree house he had made for the men to sleep in at night.

As she looked down at the sight below, Jim's words came back to Betty: "He is no fool who gives what he cannot keep, to gain what he cannot lose."

Yes, she thought, *Jim has given his life, the most precious thing that he had to give, but he has traded it for an infinitely better life in eternity.*

Jim had died obeying God, and that was enough for Betty.

Chapter 17

Visitors

Betty and Valerie Elliot returned to their home at Shandia. Everything about the place reminded Betty of Jim: the split-bamboo bed he had made for Valerie just before leaving on Operation Auca, his journal left open on the table, his clothes—some in the laundry hamper still needing to be washed. Each day brought back painful memories, but Betty determined to carry on. There was the regular work of the mission to accomplish. She oversaw the maintenance of the airstrip and the school buildings, taught at the girls' school, and continued where Jim had left off translating the Gospel of Luke into Quichua.

Sometimes Betty wondered whether Jim had had a premonition that he would die. He had worked so hard before Operation Auca to hand over leadership to the local Christian men. And now the locals took on much of the responsibility for the local fellowship and boys' school.

News of the five missionaries who had died at Palm Beach while trying to make contact with the Aucas quickly spread around the world. The deaths were reported in *Time* magazine, and a lengthy article accompanied by photos by Cornell Capa of the rescue mission appeared in *Life* magazine. With all this publicity, letters began arriving at Shandia from around the world, many from people Betty did not know. Most of the letters were comforting, but some of them offered all sorts of suggestions and ideas as to what Betty should do next.

One woman enclosed sixty dollars with her letter so that Betty could buy Bibles for the Aucas. The woman appeared to have no idea that the Aucas could not read any language or that the Auca language had never been written down. Another person wrote to say that he felt that all would be well if Betty would just write out the Ten Commandments and drop them from an airplane over Auca territory. Surely then these Indians would understand that the Word of God said, "Thou shalt not kill."

The most opinionated letters Betty received were about what should happen to Valerie now that her father was dead. Some people felt that Valerie should be returned immediately to the United States, as she was in harm's way in Ecuador. As Valerie's mother, Betty took these warnings seriously, but in the end she decided to trust God in the situation.

Rather than make her bitter or angry, Jim's death had made Betty feel more compassion than ever for the Aucas. She often found herself telling those who asked how she felt toward the Aucas, "The fact that Jesus Christ died for all makes me interested in the salvation of all, but the fact that Jim loved and died for the Aucas intensifies my love for them."

As time went on, Betty began to wonder what this love for the Aucas would eventually translate into. Somewhere in the back of her mind she had the idea that one day she and Valerie might be able to go and live with them, but for now that seemed impossible.

Meanwhile, the other widows of Operation Auca were getting on with their lives. Olive Fleming, the youngest of the widows, returned to the United States to live. Barbara Youderian and her two children stayed on at Macuma. Marj Saint stayed put at Shell Mera until MAF could send another pilot to Ecuador to replace Nate. After that she planned to move with her children to Quito to run the World Radio Missionary Fellowship missionary guesthouse. And Marilou McCully immediately flew home to Pontiac, Michigan, where she gave birth to a son two weeks later.

February 27, 1956, was a bittersweet day for Betty when Valerie turned one year old. Betty was delighted with the lovely little girl that Valerie was becoming, but she wished that Jim could be there to see their daughter grow up. She knew it would be the first of many milestones in Valerie's life where her father's absence would leave a gaping hole.

A month later Betty's mother and Mrs. DuBose from the Hampden DuBose Academy came to visit Betty and Valerie at Shandia. Katherine Howard told her daughter that she had come to see how Betty was coping with Jim's death. Betty was thrilled to see both her mother and Mrs. DuBose. The two women had meant much to her and had taught her much over the years. Their words and helping hands encouraged her to continue her missionary work, even though she desperately missed having Jim at her side.

Soon after the killings at Palm Beach, the five widows designated Betty to write an official account of the tragedy. Betty set to work on the project. Drawing heavily on both Jim and Nate's private diaries, she traced the events that led up to the men traveling to Palm Beach, and then she tried to piece together the events at Palm Beach and the killing of the men. Some of the photographs from Nate's waterlogged camera were salvaged, and journal entries from the camp helped fill in the missing pieces. The account came together quickly, and Betty was soon sending off the finished manuscript to the publisher. In August 1956 the book titled *Through Gates of Splendor* was published.

Eventually another missionary couple came to Ecuador to help with the work at Shandia. With their arrival, Betty began to feel that it was time to move on from Shandia. But where? Then one day in May 1957, Johnny Keenan flew supplies into Shandia, stopping to chat with Betty. Their conversation quickly turned to the Aucas.

"Would you like to come with me on a bucket drop to the Aucas?" Johnny asked.

Betty was aware that even after the death of the men at Palm Beach, the MAF pilots had continued to fly over the Auca settlements and use the spiral-line technique that Nate had developed to send down gifts to the Aucas. She jumped at the opportunity to fly with Johnny on one of these drops. She quickly arranged for one of her Quichua friends to babysit Valerie and climbed into the plane beside Johnny. Soon they were airborne and headed toward Auca territory. They flew over two Auca settlements but saw no one on the ground. At the third settlement they flew over, they saw a young man standing in the clearing by a thatched house. Immediately Johnny banked the plane into a tight circle and instructed Betty to feed out the line attached to the bucket. In the bucket was a hamburger, and when the bucket reached the ground, the Auca man took the hamburger from it and began to eat. He waved up to the plane between bites to acknowledge the gift.

As Betty and Johnny headed back to Shandia, Betty's heart soared higher than the airplane. Now, sixteen months after the killing of the men at Palm Beach, perhaps the Aucas were ready for another visit, or even to have missionaries come and live with them. It was hard to tell, but Betty hoped so. Her hopes were quickly dashed a few months later when a hut that Dr. Tidmarsh had built on the Curaray River was sacked. The door to the hut was ripped off, everything inside was stolen, and two lances were left at the scene as a warning to anyone who came near the location again.

After the killings at Palm Beach, Dr. Tidmarsh and his wife had moved to Arajuno. During the weekends Dr. Tidmarsh stayed with his wife in the McCullys' old house, and during the week he went to the hut he had built on the Curaray. The hut was built right at the edge of Auca territory, where Dr. Tidmarsh hoped to continue the work of making contact with the Aucas. Of course, the sacking of the hut by the Aucas was a setback to his work.

A month after the attack on the hut, Betty and Valerie visited the Tidmarshes at Arajuno. During their visit, some astonishing news unfolded. Three Auca women had walked out of the jungle at a Quichua village on the Curaray River a few miles from Arajuno. The messenger who brought the news to Arajuno did not know what the women wanted, but he did not think that they had violence on their minds. He asked Dr. Tidmarsh what the Quichua villagers should do.

Dr. Tidmarsh turned to Betty, whose heart raced as she realized this was what she had been waiting for, preparing for, since Jim's death twenty-two months before. After a brief conversation with the Tidmarshes, it was agreed that Betty should go to the village with the messenger to find out more. Mrs. Tidmarsh would watch Valerie, since there was no way Betty could carry a child that distance.

Within an hour Betty had filled a bag with everything she thought she might need: notebooks, pencils, insect repellent, soap, a snakebite kit, a change of clothes, a light blanket, and her camera. She did not take any food or a cooking pot with her, trusting that the Quichuas would share what they had with her.

The trail was arduous. Betty and the messenger scrambled up and down ravines to cross rivers and streams and jumped from boulder to boulder along the river's edge. Eventually they reached the small Quichua outpost at the edge of the Curaray River. When they arrived, two of the Auca women were still there; the third had returned to the jungle.

The Quichuas of the village kept a careful eye on the Auca newcomers. Two old Quichua grandmothers held the women's hands and tried to reassure them that they were safe, that no one wanted to harm them, and they need not be afraid. Of course, the two Auca women could not understand a word the Quichua women were saying, but Betty could see that holding their hands was reassuring to the women.

When the two Auca women saw Betty, they gasped in terror. Betty stepped back a little, realizing that they had probably never seen a white woman before. She wanted to give the Auca women a chance to observe that she was not armed and was friendly. It also gave her a chance to observe them. By now the two women were dressed in Quichua clothes, the usual straight navy blue skirt and a checkered blouse. But they wore their hair in the fringed Auca hairstyle and had the distinctive holes in their earlobes from balsa wood plugs.

After a while, the two Auca women began to relax and even allowed Betty to approach them. Betty was shocked to recognize one of the women—she was the older woman who had been on Palm Beach before Jim and the others were killed. She knew the woman's face from the photos developed from the film in Nate's camera; the images were now burned into Betty's mind.

Betty tried not to tremble as she reached out to touch hands with the Auca women. This was a strange and special moment for her.

Soon the two Auca women appeared to be completely comfortable with Betty's presence. They listened to the ticking of her watch and were delighted when she turned on her flashlight. They even "sang" a monotone chant for her, and Betty could decipher only one sound—a long, drawn-out vowel sound.

The Auca chant went on and on, and many of the Quichuas became restless.

"Maybe they are calling the men to war," one Quichua man suggested.

"Or they are casting a spell on us," another chimed in.

When night fell, all eyes were on the Auca women. Betty expected the women to leave the village, but they indicated that they wanted to spend the night. They were shown to a small room in one of the older women's houses, where they lay down to sleep.

The Quichuas of the village became very nervous as darkness enveloped the settlement, and Betty couldn't blame them. No one really knew why the women had come. The villagers wondered whether they had been sent as a distraction so that the Aucas could unexpectedly attack the village. The Quichua men slept with their guns and lances beside them and leapt to their feet at the slightest sound. "Aucas!" they would yell, before realizing that what they had heard was a dog barking or a monkey disturbing a branch above.

Betty slept on and off through the night, praying that God would show her how to proceed with this strange circumstance that had presented itself. She knew that one wrong move on her part could scare the Auca women away for good.

As the next day dragged on, a sense of foreboding hung over the settlement. Many villagers still questioned why the Auca women were there. Fortunately, in the afternoon, Dr. Tidmarsh arrived at the village with a tape recorder. Betty was happy to fill him in on the details of what had gone on thus far.

Like Betty, Dr. Tidmarsh had a keen interest in the Auca language. He demonstrated for the two Auca women how the tape recorder worked, and the older of the two appeared to understand immediately. She picked up the microphone and began talking into it. No one had any idea what she was saying, but she did not appear to care. She talked on and on, waving her hands, pointing with her chin, laughing, and flinging her head back as she spoke. It was quite a show, one that Betty wished she could have understood.

Days went by, and Betty and Dr. Tidmarsh continued to collect data on the language. The Auca women showed no signs of wanting to leave, and eventually Betty had to decide what to do next. Her work at Shandia had come to a natural end, and the two Auca women had settled in with the Quichua and appeared ready to continue speaking in their language to her so that she could write down as much of it as possible.

Betty's choice about what to do seemed obvious. She returned to Shandia, packed a few items, and commissioned a group of Quichua men to carry her things back to the settlement by the Curaray River. She had a special wooden chair made for Valerie for the journey, a chair that could be strapped to the back of one of the porters. And so Betty and Valerie joined the Auca women at the Quichua village deep in the jungle. They had been there only one day and were bathing in the river when a cry came from the village. "Aucas!"

Betty grabbed Valerie and listened.

"They've already killed! Honorio is dead. Get out of the river, señora, quickly. The Aucas are coming!"

The men of the village were off hunting at the time—all except Dario. Betty watched as Dario came thundering through the undergrowth, heading west toward the hunting party. One of the Auca women raced after him while the other sat motionless on a rock by the river.

As Betty hurriedly dressed herself and Valerie, she felt sure that the two women understood what was going on. If it was an Auca attack, there was nowhere to hide. Betty decided that it would be safer for her and Valerie in the open rather than in the jungle and stayed put where she was. No more commotion followed, and after about half an hour she carried Valerie back to the cluster of thatched huts that made up the village.

Just as night began to fall, the hunting party returned, carrying with them Honorio's body, which was riddled with eighteen spears. Some of the spears were decorated, one with some pages from a New Testament and another with the cloth cover of a scrapbook that Mrs. Tidmarsh had made for a bucket drop.

More bad news followed. Honorio's young wife had been with her husband at the time of the attack, but now she was nowhere to be found. The Quichuas were certain that the Aucas would have taken her away. Betty had no reason to doubt them.

That night Betty did some soul-searching. She felt that she and Valerie were safe—not in the sense that they could not be hurt, kidnapped, or killed but safe in the hands of God, knowing that whatever happened to them was their destiny. Still, by morning it was apparent that no one wanted the two Auca women to stay a day longer in the village. Using the few Auca words she had learned, and with lots of gestures, Betty explained to the two women that she wanted to take them back to Arajuno and then on to Shandia. The two agreed to go with her. By now they had told Betty their names: Mintaka and Maengamo.

Some Quichua Christians at Shandia offered to house the two Auca women as well as Betty and Valerie. The first few days there were hectic. Both Quichuas and white people who wanted to finally see a real, live Auca for themselves came to visit Mintaka and Maengamo.

When things settled down a little, Betty was able to get back to studying the Auca language. The work was painfully slow. Many English words had absolutely no Auca equivalent. Betty wondered what to do about abstract words like love and commitment, and concrete ones like sheep and temple. Worst of all, though, was the women's insistence that Betty could already understand Auca words and all she needed to do was listen.

Betty realized that this belief stemmed from the fact that the two women had never before encountered anyone who did not speak and understand their language and they assumed that it was spoken, or at least understood, all over the world.

The two women gave Betty an Auca name, Gikari, which means "woodpecker." Betty could never get to the bottom of why they called her this, but she liked the name anyway. It reminded her of her father's love of birds.

As the months rolled by, tape recordings of Mintaka and Maengamo talking were sent off to the United States. At the time, Rachel Saint was in the United States with Dayuma, her Auca language informant. Betty wanted Dayuma to listen to the tapes and translate them for her so that she could get a better understanding of the language.

Betty was as amazed as Rachel had been when she learned that the two Auca women talking on the tape were actually Dayuma's aunts. Soon tape-recorded conversations were flowing back and forth between Dayuma and her aunts.

Then in July 1958, Betty received some welcome news. Rachel and Dayuma were back in the Oriente and staying at Limoncocha, situated in the jungle thirty miles north of the Rio Napo and close to Auca territory. Wycliffe Bible Translators' new operational headquarters for Ecuador was located there, and once she had settled in, Rachel invited Betty to bring Mintaka and Maengamo to stay at Limoncocha with them.

As soon as the airplane pulled to a halt at the end of the airstrip at Limoncocha, Mintaka and Maengamo burst out to greet Dayuma. Betty could scarcely believe the speed at which the Auca women spoke. Their speech was rapid-fire, as if the words were being shot from a machine gun.

The three Auca women had a lot to talk about. They sat under a kapok tree and talked late into the night, reliving old times and catching each other up on what they had done since leaving the tribe. They were up again at first light, back under the kapok tree talking some more.

For their part, Betty and Rachel were able to compare language notes and solve some of the problems they each were having untangling the Auca language and reducing it to writing.

In the end, the five women all spent two months together at Limoncocha. Then one day Mintaka, Maengamo, and Dayuma came and spoke with Betty and Rachel.

"I promised my people I would come back when the kapok is ripe. It is ripe now," Maengamo said. "I am leaving. I am going home."

"What will you do when you get there?" Betty asked.

"I will say to my brother, 'Don't be afraid. I have lived with Gikari; she is good. She does not kill. Do not kill her. I will bring her to live with us. She will show us God's carvings.' I will tell them to clear the land for a woodbee [airplane], build Gikari a house. And not to be afraid. Do not lie, do not kill, do not be afraid."

The next day the three Auca women were still adamant that they were leaving, and Betty and Rachel helped them plan. It was agreed that Betty and Valerie would fly with them to Arajuno and send them on their way home from there.

It was a hard parting for Betty as she watched the three Auca women who had become her friends walk off the edge of the Arajuno airstrip and into the jungle. She prayed fervently that they would soon come back for her.

Chapter 18

At Home with the Waorani

September 25, 1958, was a bright, sunny day in the Oriente. Marj Saint was visiting Betty at Shandia. She had traveled down from Quito, where she now ran the missionary guesthouse at World Radio Missionary Fellowship. The two women sat inside Betty's small but comfortable hut and talked leisurely. Marj told Betty all about running the guesthouse in Quito, about how her children loved the city, and about the odd assortment of people who passed through the guesthouse. Of course, Marj wanted to know about Betty's encounter with the Auca women, and Betty filled her in on all the details. They then discussed Betty's new book, *Shadow of the Almighty*, which had just been published. Betty explained that she had found such a rich depository of fact, inspiration, and meditation in Jim's diary entries. In this book she had gone back and told about more of Jim's life, using his diary entries and letters as a foundation for the text.

It was late morning when Betty gathered up their coffee cups and then headed outside. As she lay her newly washed clothes on the grass to dry in the sun, she looked up and saw three Quichua women nervously approaching her. "Welcome," she said. "What brings you here?"

"Nothing. We have come for no reason," one of the Quichua women replied.

Betty nodded. She had learned that this was the standard greeting, even if they had something very important to report. "Have you seen the Aucas?" she asked the three women.

"Yes! Several of them have just come out of the jungle about half an hour's walk from here," one of the women said, pointing in the direction beyond the airstrip.

Betty raced into action. "Marj," she yelled as she ran toward her hut, "the Aucas have returned. Let's go!"

Betty grabbed her camera, scooped up Valerie, and headed toward the airstrip, with Marj close on her heels. They were partway down the airstrip when Betty heard the unmistakable sound of singing—in English!

"Jesus loves me, this I know, for the Bible tells me so."

Betty instantly recognized Dayuma's voice. Dayuma had returned for them!

Betty watched with elation as three women, Dayuma, Mintaka, and Maengamo, broke through the tall grass at the edge of the airstrip. Betty counted four more Auca women and two boys trailing behind them.

When she saw Betty, Maengamo raced to her and enveloped her in a big hug. Soon everyone was gathered around Betty and Marj, and the introductions began.

Betty then led the odd-looking assortment of naked and nearly naked people back to her hut. Before she had even finished feeding them, word had spread that the Aucas were back, and a small crowd of Quichuas gathered outside Betty's hut. The crowd grew as the afternoon progressed. The Auca group stayed the night with Betty, and in the morning still more people were peering into her hut.

Betty had to admit that it was entertaining to see these Stone Age people encounter modernity for the first time. The Aucas were fascinated with electric lights; the "fire in a box" (wood stove); the music that Betty made on her tiny portable organ; and the big, throbbing noise of the generator engine that kicked in twice a day.

The Quichua Christians at Shandia who had followed Betty's story and knew that these were members of the tribe that had murdered their missionary were very generous. They brought gifts of bananas, sugarcane, eggs, and manioc for the guests. Betty was delighted to learn that Maruja, the kidnapped wife of Honorio, whom the Aucas had killed, had been set free. The group had returned Maruja to her mother-in-law en route to Shandia. Surely that was a good sign!

As they talked into the night, Betty learned why Maengamo, Mintaka, and Dayuma had come back. The Aucas of the Curaray had invited Betty, Valerie, and Rachel to come and live with them.

"We told them you were not cannibals, and we made them believe us," Maengamo told Betty.

Betty agreed that this was a good start.

On October 6, 1958, Betty, Valerie, and Rachel, along with the nine Aucas and five Quichua porters, set out. Each porter had a gun strapped over his shoulder. This was one of the best and one of the worst days of her life as Betty watched Valerie's little blonde head bobbing up and down in the backpack chair ahead of her. Betty was excited that finally, after so much prayer, effort, and sacrifice, they were headed to an Auca settlement—and at the Aucas' invitation.

But Betty's worst fears were stirred up when they stopped to visit Maruja at her mother-in-law's house. The Aucas had held Maruja captive for a year, and Betty was eager to hear what she had to say about their possibility for success. Maruja was blunt. "Before long you will all be dead and eaten by vultures!" she said.

Betty pressed Maruja. "But did you learn to love the Aucas?"

Maruja shook her head. "The women, yes, but not the men. They are fierce. You cannot love them."

At the Curaray River, the group took canoes downstream and then followed the Añangu River upstream to the Tiwaeno River. When the river got too shallow for the canoes, they set out on foot again for the last leg of the journey. It took them two days, and as she traveled, Betty wondered whether she had done the right thing, especially bringing Valerie with her. If the adults were all killed, it could be years before word got out. Betty did not like to think about what might happen to her only child in such a case. She trekked on, trusting that God was watching over her and Valerie and Rachel.

Eventually, late in the afternoon, the group rounded a bend in the trail, and there was an Auca settlement, a small cluster of thatched huts set in a clearing in the jungle. An Auca man, naked except for a strip of cotton cloth tied around his waist, stood on a log and watched the group approach. Several women stood at the entrances to the thatched huts. They all stared as the group approached the village. Betty breathed deeply as she walked past the man and into the village. Finally she was standing in an Auca settlement. She had seen such settlements from the air, but now she was on the ground in the midst of one.

Soon Betty, Valerie, and Rachel were being introduced. Dayuma introduced Betty to her sister Gimari. Betty recognized her immediately. Gimari had visited the men at Palm Beach the day before they were killed. Betty had seen her in the photos developed from Nate's camera. And Maengamo introduced Betty to the man who had stood on the log and watched them enter the village. "This is Gikari, my brother."

At first the Quichua guides were nervous. All they knew of the Aucas was that they were brutal killers. But as everyone was introduced, the tension they felt began to lessen. It was too late in the afternoon for them to begin their return trip, so the Quichuas cautiously agreed to spend the night in the Auca village. As far as Betty knew, this was the first time in history that the Aucas had offered hospitality to strangers. At least she hoped it was hospitality.

Everyone gathered around the fire and shared a meal of fish, and then the Quichua Christians began singing some of the hymns that Jim had composed for them. It was a surreal moment for Betty. Here she was, sitting with some of the men who had undoubtedly helped in the murder of her husband, watching them as they listened intently to songs about God's love that one of the men they killed had written. Betty realized that the Aucas had never before heard music like this or words in a language other than their own. In fact, this was most likely the first time they had ever been near a person who was not in their tribe—except to spear him.

As darkness fell, the missionary women were offered "houses." Rachel was invited to stay in a hut with Maengamo and Gikita, her husband. Gikita was the oldest man in the group, and Betty judged him to be about forty-five years old. She soon learned that it was rare for an Auca to reach the age of forty—most of them came to a violent end long before then.

Betty and Valerie were offered a "house" beside Gikita's. It did not take Betty long to move in. The house consisted of four upright poles with a thatched roof. It had no covered floor or walls, and absolutely no privacy. Betty slung her few possessions into the rafters. Someone offered her a hammock, and she and Valerie slept together in it the first night.

At daybreak the following morning, Betty listened as the settlement came to life. She could hear the sound of girls filling clay water pots at the river while Gimari sang a low chant as she crouched by the fire and stirred it back to life. As the first rays of the sun began to peek through the kapok and ironwood trees that surrounded the village, birds sang and monkeys chattered.

The Quichua guides planned to leave on the return trip home early in the afternoon, and before they left, they made Valerie a simple bamboo platform bed and a table for Betty. There was no chair to go with it, but at least it provided a place off the ground for Betty to prepare Valerie's powdered milk drinks.

Finally the Quichuas said goodbye and set out for home, leaving Betty, Valerie, and Rachel alone for the first time. Betty tried not to think about the fact that the men on Palm Beach had had friendly contact with the Aucas the day before they were killed.

Betty's fears were not realized, and Betty was surprised at how quickly her new life found a rhythm of its own. In the morning she would lie in her hammock, taking a few notes and listening to everyone waking up and greeting one another. Then there was breakfast to prepare. She tried to eat like the Aucas as much as possible but supplemented her and Valerie's diet with a few Western foods. She had also brought plates and spoons with her to eat from and washed them in the river after each meal. The Aucas ate their food off palm leaves with their fingers and laughed at her constant need to wash plates and utensils.

Once the morning "housework" was taken care of, it was time for Betty to get to some serious language study. She would listen to the people talk and write down phonetically what she heard. She tried to isolate the sounds that made up the language so that the sounds could eventually be reduced to a fixed, written alphabet. One thing she learned as she studied the language was that the Aucas did not call themselves by that name. That was the name outsiders had given them. Instead, they referred to themselves as the Waorani.

During the day, Betty and Rachel went their own ways and would meet together in the evening to compare language notes and discuss what they had learned about Waorani culture. During the afternoon, Betty would often take Valerie to the garden clearing, where yucca and bananas grew. On their way back to the village they would gather wood for the fire.

All the while, Betty watched for signs of danger, but she did not see any. Dayuma had told her not to ask about Jim's death, in case the men thought she was trying to figure out who it was she should take revenge on. So Betty left that subject alone.

It was obvious from the stories Betty heard around the fire at night that the Waorani were caught in a sad cycle of killing. One of Rachel's first jobs was to put together a family tree. She told Betty that she estimated Dayuma had two hundred relatives when she had left the tribe twelve years before, and now one hundred sixty of them were dead—most of them killed in revenge killings. Betty prayed that the introduction of the gospel to the Waorani would be instrumental in breaking this cycle of killing.

Betty was amazed at how well Dayuma complemented her and Rachel's skills. Because neither of the missionaries was yet fluent in Waorani, Dayuma took on the role of missionary to her own people. She taught them how to count off the days in lots of seven so that on the seventh day they could have a holy day. She also got the people together and taught them from God's carvings (the Bible) and made up simple hymns for them to learn.

Prayer was one of the hardest things for the Waorani to grasp. They had no idea what it meant to pray, and people would often close their eyes, bow their heads, and nod right off to sleep. Of course, Dayuma was right there to prod them awake again.

Bit by bit, some of the tribe began to respond to the gospel. No one but Dayuma was yet a Christian, but the people began to ask thoughtful questions about God.

After two months at the Waorani settlement on the Tiwaeno River, Betty and Valerie left to visit Jim's parents, who were waiting for them in Quito. This was the first time the Elliots had met their grand-daughter. They all spent a happy Christmas together in Quito, and after Jim's parents left, Betty stayed on for a much-needed break.

Meanwhile, Rachel and Dayuma also took a break from the harsh reality of living in the jungle. The two of them traveled back to Limoncocha.

Betty and Valerie returned to the Tiwaeno settlement in March 1959, and Rachel and Dayuma had arrived back at the village several weeks before them. They resumed their language work and shared the gospel with the Waorani at every chance they got.

Time passed slowly in the jungle, and the everyday tasks of living took up much more time than Betty wanted them to. Still, along with keeping up her missionary work, Betty managed to keep a detailed journal of her life and the events at Tiwaeno.

In September 1959, Betty once again left the Waorani behind, this time returning home to New Jersey. After eight years away, being home was quite a culture shock for her. The American economy seemed to be booming, and new houses and roads were springing up everywhere. On what had once been rural land now sat suburbs with neat, single-story homes that lined paved streets. New Jersey presented even more of a culture shock for Valerie, who had been born and had lived her young life in the jungle.

Back in the United States, Betty found herself somewhat of a Christian celebrity. Her two books, *Through Gates of Splendor* and *The Shadow of the*

Almighty, were both best-sellers. As a result, Betty had the opportunity to speak at many churches and Christian gatherings, where she urged people to look beyond their own circumstances and see God's plan for their lives.

While Betty was at home, an editor from her publisher met with her and reviewed the photographs she had taken of her seven-month experience in the jungle with the Waorani. The editor asked her to write the text for a book to go along with the photos. Betty agreed to do so, even though it would delay her return to the Waorani. The title of the book was *The Savage My Kinsman.*

When Betty and Valerie finally returned to the Waorani, they discovered that many changes had taken place. Rachel had stayed on in Tiwaeno while Betty was away, and she had made substantial progress. A number of the Waorani in the settlement had become Christians, including several of the men who had taken part in the killing of the missionary men at Palm Beach.

Another big change had occurred too. The Waorani had cleared away a swath of the jungle between the river and the village for an airstrip. Betty had the privilege of standing beside the airstrip when Don Smith, the local JAARS (Jungle Aviation and Radio Service) pilot who serviced the workers with Wycliffe Bible Translators throughout the Oriente, brought his plane in to land at the airstrip for the first time. Now a trip to Arajuno, which used to take up to three days trekking through the jungle, took only ten minutes.

Despite the many advances, things did not go smoothly for Betty upon her return to Tiwaeno. While Betty was away, Rachel had lived alone, without any other Europeans. As a result, Rachel had come to a different understanding of the way forward in the village. And she was now much farther along in the study of the Waorani language than Betty was and had already begun some Bible translation into the language.

The two headstrong missionary women began to clash. Despite both of their best efforts to get along, the relationship wore Betty down. It was easy to see that the two of them were not working together, and Betty concluded it would be best for her to leave. This was not a quick decision, but once she had made it, Betty felt confident that it was the right thing to do.

Before she left, though, Betty had the joy of witnessing the first Waorani baptism. Dr. Everett Fuller from the medical clinic at Shell Mera agreed to make weekly visits to the community to take care of the various health needs of the Waorani. On his first visit to Tiwaeno, Dr. Fuller baptized nine Waorani believers in the river. Tears welled in Betty's eyes as she watched the event. How she wished Jim and the others could have been there to see the baptism, which represented the fulfillment of what they had given their lives for.

Soon after the baptism, Betty attended Dayuma's wedding. Dayuma married Komi, one of the recently baptized believers. Once again Betty was profoundly touched as she watched the event.

Finally it was time for Betty and Valerie, now six years old, to leave. It did not take Betty long to pack their belongings, since she had very little to take with her—just her journals, camera, film, and a few clothes.

Although it was sad saying goodbye to the Waorani of Tiwaeno, Betty knew that leaving was the right thing to do. As she made her way out of the jungle, Betty thought about the remarkable time spent among her husband's killers, with all of its heartaches and joys. She wondered what was in store for her next.

Chapter 19

Elisabeth Elliot

After leaving Tiwaeno and the Waorani, Betty went back to work among the Quichua Indians for a time. Then in 1963, after having served for eleven years as a missionary in Ecuador, Betty left the country with Valerie and returned to the United States. Back home, Betty's life was soon caught up in a flurry of activity. Many churches and Christian groups wanted to hear Betty speak. Betty began traveling the country, speaking and challenging people about missions and the need to live pure and godly Christian lives. The more she spoke, the more popular she became. Betty quickly began to enjoy her new ministry role as a traveling speaker.

In the summer of 1963, Betty's parents retired and moved to Vero Beach, Florida. They had barely settled in when her father died suddenly on Christmas Day. Betty and Valerie went to comfort Mrs. Howard, but Betty's mother was radiant. "Apart from a few tears, my heart is full of nothing but thankfulness," she declared.

Betty felt the same way. Her father had been a strong and consistent godly influence in her life, and she realized that she owed a lot to him for that. However, the experience of losing a parent underscored to Betty the importance of writing down memories before they were lost forever. It was now too late to capture all the things her father remembered, but Betty urged her mother to buy a notebook and start writing down the experiences that she recalled from her life, along with things she wanted to say to the next generation.

At the same time, people were encouraging Betty herself to write more about her experiences. In this regard, Betty was grateful that she had been keeping a journal since the age of sixteen. Her journal provided plenty of material to draw on as she wrote—and write she did. Her first attempt was a novel she titled *No Graven Images*. The story was about a single missionary woman who goes to live among the Quichua Indians in Ecuador and encounters many discouragements along the way. Of course, much of the plot was based on personal experiences from Betty's life. Betty wanted to show Christians that a person can be in God's will and still have things go terribly "wrong." By that, Betty meant things could be going wrong from the person's perspective but that those things could well be part of God's plan to bless the person and make him or her more Christlike. The novel was published in 1966, and its message was difficult for some Christians to read, but they respected Betty's own journey through her missionary endeavors and the death of her husband.

By now Betty was going by her full name of Elisabeth Elliot when she was out speaking. It made more sense to her to be introduced at a meeting by the name that was also on the cover of her books. As Betty's speaking and writing continued, invitations came in for her to speak in places near and far. At one such speaking engagement in 1968, Betty met Dr. Addison Leitch, who was recently widowed and taught theology at seminary level. Betty felt immediately drawn to him. She soon learned that Addison had a PhD from Cambridge University and was a regular columnist for the prestigious *Christianity Today* magazine. He was also a very athletic man. He coached swimming and football and loved baseball.

Addison and Betty saw each other several times, and then in October 1968, Addison proposed marriage to Betty, who joyfully accepted his proposal. She was forty-two years old and had been a widow now over twelve years. Addison was eighteen years older than Betty.

The couple were married on New Year's Day 1969, with Valerie as Betty's attendant. Following the wedding they moved to Hamilton, Massachusetts, where Addison was a professor at the newly formed Gordon-Conwell Theological Seminary.

Addison encouraged Betty to continue with her writing and speaking. Betty was in constant demand as a speaker, and over half a million of her books were now in print.

Life with Addison in Hamilton was good. However, on New Year's Day 1973, their fourth wedding anniversary, Addison and Betty received some bad news. Addison was diagnosed with not one but two separate forms of cancer. The outlook for his making a full recovery was not good. By now Valerie was away in Illinois in her freshman year at Wheaton College, and Betty had to bear the full weight of caring for her sick husband. Addison underwent surgery and both chemotherapy and radiation therapy. Sometimes he was in such excruciating pain that he screamed out in agony for help.

Betty was devastated to watch her husband's condition. She tried to assure herself that this was God's assignment for them and that she had to leave the outcome in His hands.

When she realized just how much work was involved in helping her sick husband, Betty advertised for a theology student to come and board at the house who could stay with Addison on those times when she had to leave the house. A young man named Walter Shepard answered the advertisement. On the same day that Walter moved into the house in September 1973, Addison died.

Even though there was now no need for Walter's help in caring for Addison, Betty decided to invite him to stay on anyway. She realized that she would be lonely in such a big house, and having someone young around the house would help as she got used to being a widow once again.

Soon Betty heard of a second man who needed a place to stay. His name was Lars Gren, an older student who had returned to school in midlife after a career selling women's clothing. Betty took Lars in as a boarder as well. Like Walter, Lars was pursuing a Master of Divinity degree at Gordon-Conwell Theological Seminary.

This was an unusual and international group living in the big house in Hamilton. Walter was the son of missionaries to the Belgian Congo, where he had grown up. Lars had been born in the United States but had spent most of his childhood in Norway. And Betty, of course, had been born in Belgium, grew up in the United States, and had lived in South America.

At Christmas Valerie returned home for recess and finally met the young man her mother had written to her about. She and Walter got to know each other a little over the Christmas break, and Betty began to wonder whether they might be right for each other.

Betty continued with her various ministries. Her books about Jim and her ministry to the Waorani remained popular, and many people who read them wanted to know about her missionary life before she married Jim Elliot. In response, Betty delved into her diaries once more and wrote *These Strange Ashes,* an account of her year working with the Colorado Indians in the jungle of western Ecuador. She did not sugarcoat her experiences or her accomplishments, and many readers appreciated her candor in the book.

Betty's intuition about Valerie and Walter proved correct, and the couple were married on May 1, 1975. Betty was thrilled that her daughter had chosen a godly husband. Soon after Walter and Valerie were married, Walter took up a position as a Presbyterian minister at a church in southwest Louisiana.

Meanwhile, Lars obtained his Master of Divinity degree, and his goal was to become a hospital chaplain. During the time he had been boarding with Betty, however, the two had become good friends. Betty never imagined that she would marry again, but when Lars obtained his degree, he asked Betty to be his wife. It was strange for Betty to think of marrying for a third time, especially since she could not think of three more different men than Jim, Addison, and Lars, except for one thing: all three of them were dedicated to living for Christ.

Betty and Lars were married on December 21, 1977, Betty's fifty-first birthday. Lars was ten years younger than Betty. After their wedding, Lars put aside his plan to become a hospital chaplain in order to assist Betty in her ministry. What a relief it was for Betty when Lars took over the travel and financial arrangements. Betty did not realize what a burden they had become.

Betty enjoyed having Lars as her traveling companion. It was much less lonely being on the road with another person, someone she knew she would be going home with and could discuss her experiences with. Sometimes Betty would joke, "I only ever had two boarders. My daughter married one, and I married the other!"

In 1978 Valerie gave birth to a son, Walter Shepard III, making Betty a grandmother.

Betty's life continued to be busy. She was invited to be a consultant for the committee putting together the New International Version of the Bible, and she still traveled and spoke around the country. She also continued with her writing. She wrote a book about the joys of being a Christian woman, titled *Let Me Be a Woman*. She quickly followed that volume with a book of inspirational essays, titled *Love Has a Price Tag*.

In 1982 Betty ventured out into another ministry avenue. She began writing a regular newsletter called *The Elisabeth Elliot Newsletter*. Over the years people had suggested that Betty write a regular newsletter, but Betty had resisted, not wanting to be burdened with the details of getting it printed, managing a mailing list, printing labels, and mailing the newsletter. However, when Servant Publications in Ann Arbor, Michigan, offered its services in taking care of all the mechanics of putting together the newsletter and mailing it out, Betty accepted their offer. The first edition of the newsletter was published in November 1982. It included Betty's insights from the Bible, practical advice, stories about Betty's family, excerpts from letters she received, and prayer requests.

Many people wanted to be kept up to date on all of Betty's activities and subscribed to the newsletter, which was published six times a year. The popularity of the newsletter expanded Betty's influence around the world. Betty continued to travel and speak, and she especially enjoyed any opportunity to head to the southern states, which made it easy for her to visit Valerie and Walt and their growing family. When the newsletter began, Valerie had three children. Two more followed in rapid succession, making Betty a grandmother of five busy, bright grandchildren.

After starting *The Elisabeth Elliot Newsletter,* Betty enjoyed one of the biggest thrills of her life. She was asked to write a biography of her favorite writer, the Anglo-Irish missionary Amy Carmichael. From the time she was introduced to Amy Carmichael's books when she was a fourteen-year-old student at the Hampden DuBose Academy, Betty had been inspired by Amy's writing. She had read and reread the books many times and loved to quote Amy in her own books and sermons.

As part of the research for the book, Betty and Lars traveled to southern India to visit the Dohnavur Fellowship, founded by Amy Carmichael. They got to see firsthand the ongoing work of the ministry Amy had started over eighty years before. They visited the school, the dormitories, and the nurseries that housed the children at Dohnavur Fellowship. They watched the daily meals being prepared and visited the sewing room where all the children's clothes were made, the hospital, and the retirement home. Betty was impressed by the fact that the fellowship was run almost entirely by people who had been rescued as children from dire situations and had grown up at Dohnavur.

Betty and Lars spent nine enjoyable days at Dohnavur, staying in a small guest bungalow on the compound. When Betty entered Amy's bedroom, called the "Room of Peace," she felt as if she were standing on hallowed ground. She sat at the desk where Amy had penned so many of the stories, poems, and books that had enthralled Betty since childhood. Betty thought about the twenty years Amy had spent bedridden in that very room and how, despite her condition, Amy had managed to praise God for all the good things He had given her.

In fact, everything about Dohnavur inspired Betty. She found it easy to imagine many of the events she had read about in Amy's books, and she returned home to the United States invigorated and ready to get to work on the biography. When the finished biography of Amy Carmichael, titled *A Chance to Die*, was published in 1987, it became an instant best-seller.

At the same time that the Amy Carmichael biography was being published, Betty's mother died on February 7, 1987. Katharine Howard had been in declining health for three years, and on the afternoon of her death she had told her nurse that she was going to die.

The entire Howard family gathered for the funeral, the family's first gathering in many years. The funeral was a wonderful tribute to Katharine Howard. Betty joined her siblings in giving eulogies. As Betty listened to her brothers and sister speak, memories flooded back of how her mother, through her letter writing, had loved to keep in touch with her family and keep her children in touch with each other. Betty's mother had written a weekly family letter consistently for forty years. Betty's sister, Virginia, spoke about how their mother had taught her what it meant to be a lady, while her brother Tom recalled how Katharine Howard had spent hours reading and singing to them all when they were children. Betty's brother Jim spoke of seeing their mother year after year sitting in her cane rocking chair after breakfast each day reading her Bible and taking copious notes.

The funeral service concluded with all six of Katharine Howard's children singing one last hymn together in honor of their mother. Betty thought the gesture was fitting, since their mother had instilled in them all such a deep love for hymns.

After the funeral, Betty sat down and reread her mother's journals, family letters, and reminiscences. She was inspired by what she read and used the material as the basis for a new book, *The Shaping of a Christian Family*.

But there was still more for Betty to do.

Chapter 20

Gateway to Joy

Y ou are loved with an everlasting love.' That's
what the Bible says. 'And underneath are the
everlasting arms.' This is your friend Elisabeth Elliot,
talking with you today about…"

As she continued, Betty surveyed the script in
front of her and adjusted the microphone. It was
October 3, 1988, and she was beginning a whole new
adventure. It had begun several years earlier when a
young woman named Jan Anderson introduced herself to Betty at a conference in Urbana, Illinois. Soon
afterward Jan moved to Quito, Ecuador, to work with
the Christian radio station HCJB. During her time in
Quito, Jan wrote regular, long, vivid letters to Betty
about her experiences there. Eventually Jan returned
to the United States and came to a conference in

Georgia at which Betty was the featured speaker. At the end of the conference she approached Betty and said, "I have made up my mind. You need to be on the radio, and I'm going to help you get there."

True to her word, Jan approached the director of the *Back to the Bible* broadcast in Lincoln, Nebraska, and suggested that he might like to do a women's radio program. The director declared his interest in the idea if Jan could come up with the right person to host the show. Of course, Jan already had Betty Elliot in mind. The members of the board of *Back to the Bible* had read many of Betty's books and newsletters and quickly decided Betty was the right person to host the new venture, which was to be called *Gateway to Joy.*

It took some organizing to work out the details so that Betty could continue to travel as much as she did and at the same time produce five fifteen-minute broadcast segments a week. Mostly the segments were taped in the studio, but occasionally they were recorded at Betty's home.

Each radio broadcast began with the same greeting, which included lines from two of Betty's favorite verses, Jeremiah 31:3 and Deuteronomy 33:27. On the show, Betty talked about all sorts of things that she thought would interest her listeners: Bible stories, missionary stories of her own and of other people, poems and hymns that meant a lot to her, her travel adventures around the world, and updates on Valerie and the grandchildren. Betty was able to tell her listeners about the births of three more grandchildren, bringing the total number of children in the Shepard household to eight.

Gateway to Joy became a very popular radio broadcast, and with its popularity, the mail began to flow in from listeners. Betty read every letter and tried to respond to each one. She often read excerpts from the letters on the air and then answered listeners' questions. When the volume of letters became too much for one person to handle, Lars pitched in and helped Betty answer them.

Betty continued to be in demand as a speaker and traveled widely, but in January 1996 she made a very special trip. Betty and Lars, along with Valerie and Walter and grandson Walter Shepard III, went to Ecuador.

When Betty left the Waorani in 1962, Rachel Saint remained and continued to work among them. She stayed faithful to that calling until she died in 1994. When Steve Saint, Rachel's nephew and Nate Saint's son, went to Ecuador to attend his aunt's funeral, the Waorani elders asked him to bring his family and come and live with them in the jungle.

At that stage of his life, Steve was a successful businessman with a wife and four teenage children. Nonetheless, he prayed about the invitation and concluded that it was what God wanted him to do next. The Saint family moved into the jungle of the Oriente to live with the Waorani. Now, the Elliot/Gren/Shepard family was on its way to visit them.

The memories flooded back as Betty peered out the airplane window. Memories of seeing the Andes for the first time on her way to do language study in Quito, of flying to Panama on her honeymoon with Jim, and then, as a young widow, flying "home" to a new life in the United States with blonde-haired Valerie bobbing up and down in the seat beside her on the plane.

Two days after setting out, Betty and the other members of her family were crowded into Steve and Ginny Saint's house. The Saints lived in a small settlement among the Waorani. No sooner had Betty and her family arrived than a steady stream of people flowed through the house, laughing, singing, gawking, and reminiscing about old times with Betty and Valerie.

The men in the group set out on an all-day trek to visit Gikita, one of the men who had been responsible for the ambush of Jim Elliot and the other four missionaries at Palm Beach exactly forty years before.

Betty and Valerie stayed behind at the settlement to reminisce some more. They were shown around a Waorani school, where the children learned both Spanish and the Waorani language. They sang gospel songs and recited Bible verses from the Waorani translation of the New Testament, of which Betty had played an important part in the early stages, helping Rachel Saint to understand and write down the language. Now the New Testament translation into that language was complete. Betty was excited to see the progress that had been made among the Waorani.

On Sunday they attended church in the settlement. Again Betty's mind went back to the time when

Dayuma had first counted off seven days and insisted that her relatives gather and listen to her speak on the seventh day—God's Day. No one knew at the time how to pray or even how to concentrate on a story about a foreigner born two thousand years before in a far-off country. Now many in the tribe embraced that Person as their Savior.

The week among the Waorani passed quickly, but by the time she left to return home, Betty had gathered a lot of updated information to pass on to her radio listeners and newsletter readers. But much more than that, she had the satisfaction of seeing some of the results of Jim's sacrifice and her own years of effort spent in the jungle of the Oriente.

For Betty the trip was the completion of a circle. What a thrill it had been to see her grandson Walter trek seven hours through the jungle to greet his grandfather's killer, now a Christian brother, and to see Valerie and Steve regaling each other with shared memories of life as children in the jungle. And finally, too, for Lars to experience so many things that had played such a key role in shaping Betty and her ministry.

When she returned to the United States, Betty continued her rigorous ministry schedule. In the two months after getting home from the visit to Ecuador, she spoke in Birmingham, Alabama; Rutland, Vermont; Jacksonville, Oregon; Montreal, Quebec; and many points in between.

On August 31, 2001, Betty ended her *Gateway to Joy* radio program. Indeed, it had been a gateway to joy for her. She thoroughly enjoyed the opportunity to reach out to so many people in the widely syndicated show's twelve years on the radio. Thousands of people had written to her with their problems and thanked her for being part of the solution.

Two years after the final radio show, *The Elisabeth Elliot Newsletter* ceased publication, after coming out six times a year continuously for twenty-one years. At times more than eighteen thousand people in over one hundred countries read the newsletter. When writing the newsletter, Betty had always sought to raise awareness of missionaries and their work, from Peru to Egypt. And in the last ten years of the newsletter's existence, readers sent in nearly a quarter of a million dollars to help with the causes Betty had highlighted.

A month after the newsletter ceased publication, Betty turned seventy-seven years old. As hard as it was for her and Lars to admit, Betty was slipping into old age. She began to experience difficulty in saying some words and in recalling Bible verses and poems that she had quoted by heart since she was a child. Bit by bit, almost imperceptibly to others, Betty's mind and body were becoming frail.

Betty finished her official speaking and traveling ministry in 2004. She still tried her best to get to a few favorite events, but her attendance took a different form than it previously had. More often than not, Lars would show the group a video recorded at a previous event when she was younger. Afterward, Betty would answer questions or add a few words.

In May 2009, Betty tripped and fell, breaking her leg. Just as she was recovering from that fall, she fell again, this time breaking five small bones in her foot. The injuries required a stay in a special care facility for the elderly. As Betty was wheeled around, fed, and bathed, she and Lars faced the reality of this final stage of life. No one can say how long it will be.

Betty was finally able to leave the special care facility and with part-time help remains in her cozy home in Magnolia, Massachusetts, to where she and Lars moved from Hamilton. Betty often relies on her old "friend" Amy Carmichael, who was bedridden for twenty years, to light the way for her. In the past when she spoke of suffering, Betty often quoted the last lines of Amy's Carmichael's poem "In Acceptance Lieth Peace":

> He said, "I will accept the breaking sorrow
> Which God tomorrow
> Will to His son explain."
> Then did the turmoil deep within him cease.
> Not vain the word, not vain;
> For in acceptance lieth peace.

In her long life, Elisabeth Elliot has accepted and embraced many sorrows without complaint, and without questioning her God. She had lived her own message—a message of joyful surrender—before passing it on to the world.

Benge, Janet and Geoff. *Jim Elliot: One Great Purpose.* Seattle: YWAM Publishing, 1999.

———. *Rachel Saint: A Star in the Jungle.* Seattle: YWAM Publishing, 2005.

Elliot, Elisabeth. *Passion and Purity.* Old Tappan, N.J.: Revell, 1984.

———. *Shadow of the Almighty: The Life and Testament of Jim Elliot.* New York: Harper, 1958.

———. *The Shaping of a Christian Family.* Nashville: Oliver Nelson, 1992.

———. *These Strange Ashes.* New York: Harper & Row, 1975.

———. *The Savage My Kinsman.* New York: Harper, 1961.

———. *Through Gates of Splendor.* New York: Harper, 1957.

Miller, Susan Martins. *Jim Elliot: Missionary to Ecuador.* Uhrichsville, Ohio: Barbour, 1998.

Additional material was drawn from archived copies of *The Elisabeth Elliot Newsletter* and from transcripts of Elisabeth Elliot's *Gateway to Joy* radio broadcasts.

Janet and Geoff Benge are a husband and wife writing team with more than thirty years of writing experience. Janet is a former elementary school teacher. Geoff holds a degree in history. Originally from New Zealand, the Benges spent ten years serving with Youth With A Mission. They have two daughters, Laura and Shannon, and an adopted son, Lito. They make their home in the Orlando, Florida, area.

Also from Janet and Geoff Benge...

More adventure-filled biographies for ages 10 to 100!

Christian Heroes: Then and Now

Gladys Aylward: The Adventure of a Lifetime • 978-1-57658-019-6
Nate Saint: On a Wing and a Prayer • 978-1-57658-017-2
Hudson Taylor: Deep in the Heart of China • 978-1-57658-016-5
Amy Carmichael: Rescuer of Precious Gems • 978-1-57658-018-9
Eric Liddell: Something Greater Than Gold • 978-1-57658-137-7
Corrie ten Boom: Keeper of the Angels' Den • 978-1-57658-136-0
William Carey: Obliged to Go • 978-1-57658-147-6
George Müller: Guardian of Bristol's Orphans • 978-1-57658-145-2
Jim Elliot: One Great Purpose • 978-1-57658-146-9
Mary Slessor: Forward into Calabar • 978-1-57658-148-3
David Livingstone: Africa's Trailblazer • 978-1-57658-153-7
Betty Greene: Wings to Serve • 978-1-57658-152-0
Adoniram Judson: Bound for Burma • 978-1-57658-161-2
Cameron Townsend: Good News in Every Language • 978-1-57658-164-3
Jonathan Goforth: An Open Door in China • 978-1-57658-174-2
Lottie Moon: Giving Her All for China • 978-1-57658-188-9
John Williams: Messenger of Peace • 978-1-57658-256-5
William Booth: Soup, Soap, and Salvation • 978-1-57658-258-9
Rowland Bingham: Into Africa's Interior • 978-1-57658-282-4
Ida Scudder: Healing Bodies, Touching Hearts • 978-1-57658-285-5
Wilfred Grenfell: Fisher of Men • 978-1-57658-292-3
Lillian Trasher: The Greatest Wonder in Egypt • 978-1-57658-305-0
Loren Cunningham: Into All the World • 978-1-57658-199-5
Florence Young: Mission Accomplished • 978-1-57658-313-5
Sundar Singh: Footprints Over the Mountains • 978-1-57658-318-0
C.T. Studd: No Retreat • 978-1-57658-288-6
Rachel Saint: A Star in the Jungle • 978-1-57658-337-1
Brother Andrew: God's Secret Agent • 978-1-57658-355-5
Clarence Jones: Mr. Radio • 978-1-57658-343-2
Count Zinzendorf: Firstfruit • 978-1-57658-262-6
John Wesley: The World His Parish • 978-1-57658-382-1
C. S. Lewis: Master Storyteller • 978-1-57658-385-2
David Bussau: Facing the World Head-on • 978-1-57658-415-6
Jacob DeShazer: Forgive Your Enemies • 978-1-57658-475-0
Isobel Kuhn: On the Roof of the World • 978-1-57658-497-2
Elisabeth Elliot: Joyful Surrender • 978-1-57658-513-9
D. L. Moody: Bringing Souls to Christ • 978-1-57658-552-8
Paul Brand: Helping Hands • 978-1-57658-536-8
Dietrich Bonhoeffer: In the Midst of Wickedness • 978-1-57658-713-3
Francis Asbury: Circuit Rider • 978-1-57658-737-9

Heroes of History

Available in paperback, e-book, and audiobook formats.
Unit Study Curriculum Guides are available for many biographies.
www.YWAMpublishing.com

CHRISTIAN HEROES: THEN & NOW are available in paperback, e-book, and audiobook formats, with more coming soon!

www.HeroesThenAndNow.com